THE
CLASSICAL
MALE
FIGURE

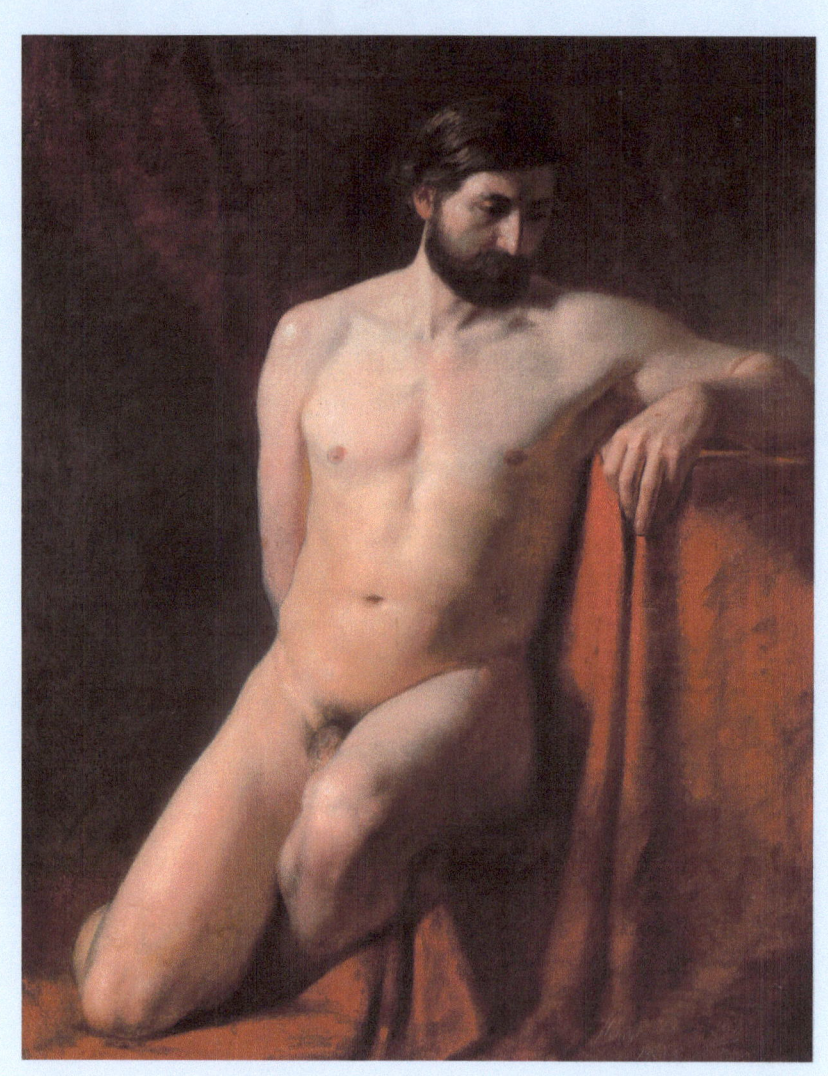

THE CLASSICAL MALE FIGURE

50 FRAMEABLE 8" x 10" PRINTS OF EXQUISITE, HISTORICAL MALE FIGURE ART

THE LIVING ROOM ART GALLERY SERIES

COMPILED & INTRODUCED BY GREG FOX

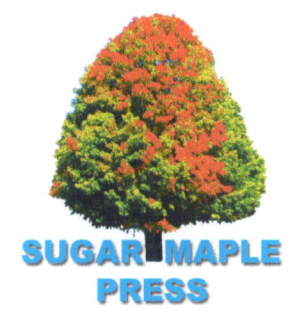

SUGAR MAPLE PRESS

OTHER BOOKS by GREG FOX

Kyle's Bed & Breakfast

Kyle's Bed & Breakfast: A Second Bowl of Serial

Kyle's Bed & Breakfast: Hot off the Griddle

Kyle's Bed & Breakfast: Without Reservations

Kyle's B&B Presents: Drawings of Drew

The Sugar Maple Press Anthology of Nature Poems (editor)

**Dedicated, with love,
to Eleanor and Sheila**

FRONT COVER: "Man Wearing Laurels" - John Singer Sargent - circa 1874-1880
BACK COVER: "Sleeping Endymion" - Nicolas-Guy Brenet - 1756
OPPOSITE TITLE PAGE: "Male Nude With a Drape" - Henryk Siemiradzki - late 19th century

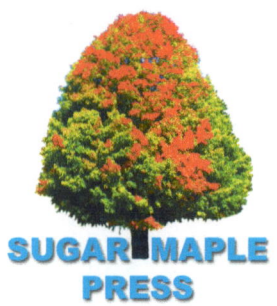

Sugar Maple Press

www.sugarmaplepress.com

e-mail: sugarmaplepress@yahoo.com

All Sugar Maple Press titles are available at special quantity discounts for bulk purchases, for sales promotions, premiums, fundraising, educational or institutional use.
Contact us at sugarmaplepress@yahoo.com for details.

ISBN-13:   978-0692655177
ISBN-10:   0692655174

First Sugar Maple Press Trade Paperback Printing: Spring, 2016

Introduction

When I launched the Classical Male Figure page on Facebook on a snowy January day in 2016, the thought of doing a book had honestly not crossed my mind. I simply wanted to have a place to post and share the wealth of beautiful historic art of the male figure...much of which has never been seen by many people alive today.

I'd attended a lecture about John Singer Sargent, one of my favorite artists, at the local library here in Northport a couple of weeks earlier. A nice talk and a fairly good power-point presentation, but no mention was made of Sargent's paintings & drawings of the male nude figure. Curious, as I believe that it is some of his most powerful and heartfelt work. Perhaps not so curious, though, as Sargent displayed hardly any of that work publicly during his lifetime. Fortunately, Sargent's sisters Emily and Violet saved the contents of his studio after his death, and donated the contents to museums to safeguard these works for future generations. But the majority of Sargent's depictions of the male nude figure retain an air of mystery to this day. (You'll be happy to know that several are featured here in this book!). Of course, the male nude figure has often been a hot-button topic in the art world. The female figure, too, has generated

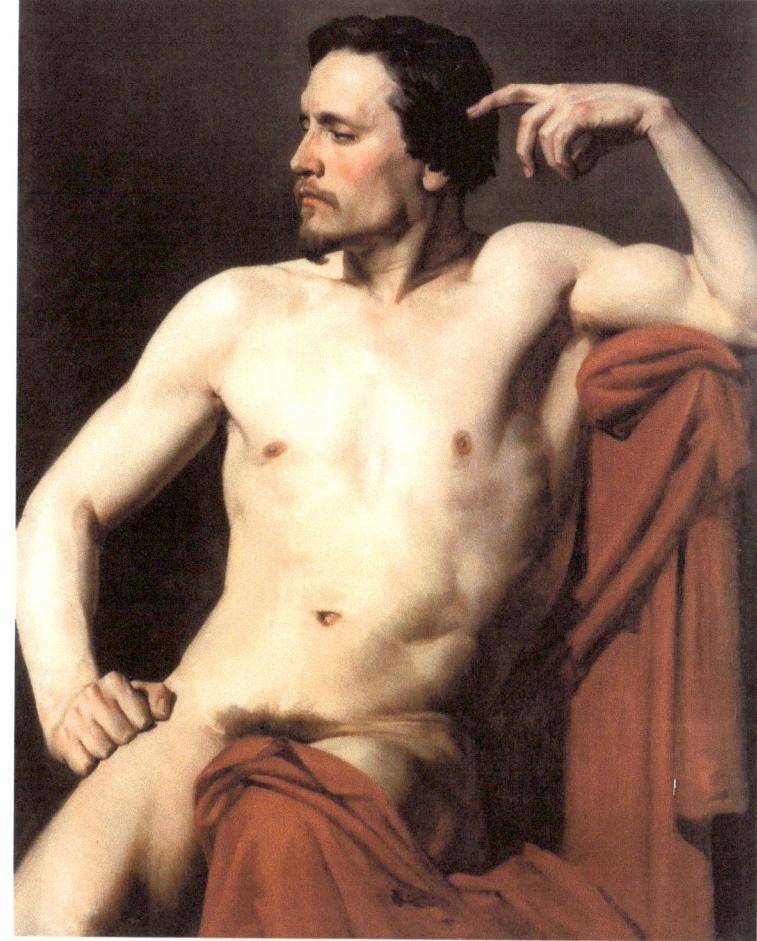

William Bouguereau - Male Nude, 1850

its own share of controversy, but something about the undraped male really seems to unhinge a good number of people. Michelangelo in the 1500s... Thomas Eakins in the 1800s... they both had their own sets of problems because of their insistence on including male nudity in their work. And this isn't something confined to history. I think every working artist today who has shown work with male nudes in it, (myself included), has at least one or two censorship stories to tell, often happening in galleries where they hadn't expected any such prudery to occur.

All of this was on my mind for days after the Sargent lecture at Northport library, and got me thinking about how brave were those artists over the past centuries who had included male nudes in their work, despite overwhelming societal pressure not to. Often, the figures were worked into mythological scenes where, somehow, nudes were given a reluctant pass. Or, thankfully, the artists were indeed allowed to paint or draw the nude male figure in their course of study, as many of the artworks in this book are described as "Academic Studies". There's something deeply moving about these respectful, classical depictions of the male nude from the Renaissance up through the Edwardian era that has always touched me when I view them. (Yes, even the ones with fig leaves and drapery covering their genitals... sometimes, even that aspect was worked into the artwork with care & creativity). It was with this inspiration that I decided to create a Facebook page dedicated to show-

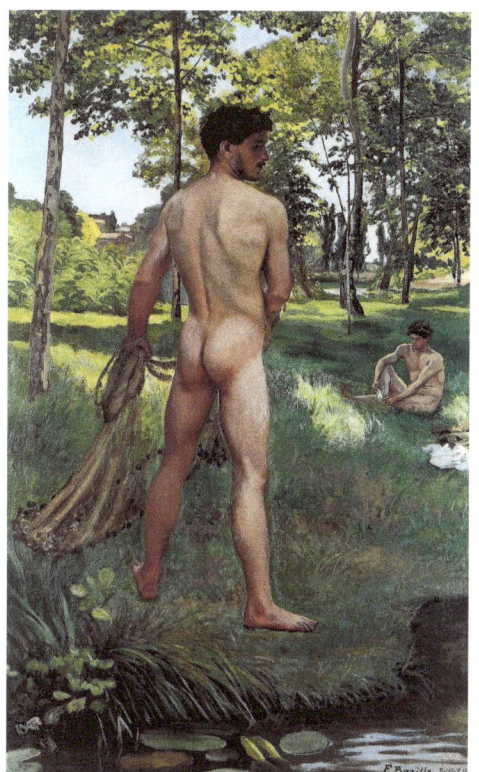

Frederic Bazille -
The Fisherman With a Net - 1868

casing the art of the classical male figure less than 2 weeks after the infamous James Singer Sargent lecture, (launching on the night of January 22nd, just as the record-breaking Blizzard of 2016 was bearing down on the east coast of the USA. Seriously. Look it up!).

Within a few weeks of launching, as more & more people began "liking" the page on Facebook, it occurred to me that:

A) A lot of people, (including me), were interested in having prints of some of these works of art, to beautify either their homes or work spaces.

B) A collection of this work, in book form, really needed to be put together.

Being that I am already in the publishing world, and that I've published 5 books so far of my comic strip **Kyle's Bed & Breakfast** through Sugar Maple Press, it was not a stretch for me to get this book project off the ground. One of those Kyle's B&B books happened to be a book of pin-up prints, so I knew that Sugar Maple Press was up to the task.

So, here it is now... 50 of what I believe are some of the most beautiful male figure artworks of that "classical era", (roughly between the Renaissance era up to about 1920). Not all of them are nudes, (though most are). While the nude male figure was my original intention with the book, as I began selecting artwork, it became more about finding the most beautiful depictions of the male form. Some of those may include occasional clothing, drapery, (or fig leaves!), but I believe they're all worthy of inclusion here. And while I did feel it important to include a few well-known classics here, (such as one of Michelangelo's Sistine Chapel "Ignudi", and also Thomas Eakins' "Swimming"), I think you'll find the majority of works here are not as well known, but certainly deserve to be. And I'm delighted to be able to bring them out of the shadows of history for new generations to appreciate.

As stated, this is a book of hang-able, frame-able prints, but you don't need to hang them. The book functions equally well as a coffee-table book, to enjoy the artwork in book form for years to come. If you do choose to hang & frame these, though, you'll be happy to know all of the works here are sized to fit into 8" x 10" frames, probably the most common, (and inexpensive), pre-made frame size. So you won't need to spend exorbitant amounts of money having any custom

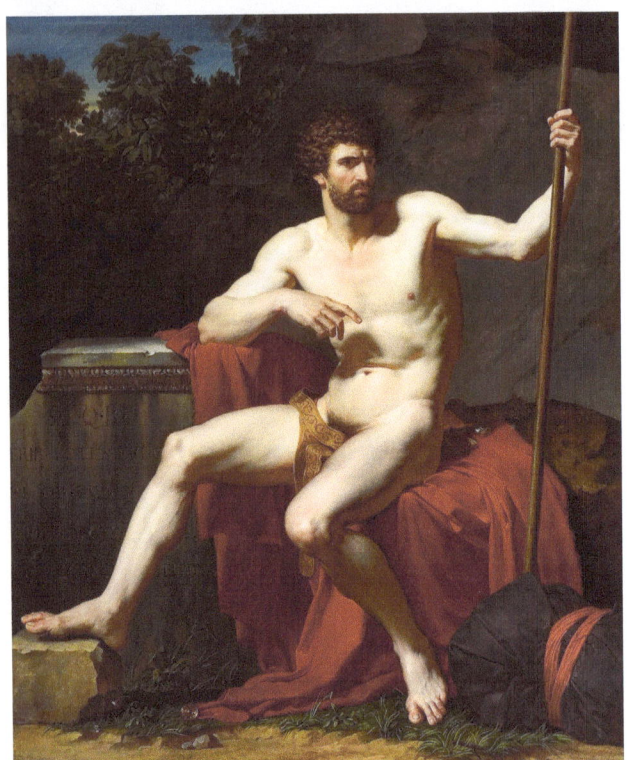

Francois Xavier Fabre - Roman Soldier at Rest - 1788

frames made for these prints. (Tips on how to remove prints from this book, and also tips on where to buy low-cost, quality frames, are on page 107 at the back of this book).

I hope you enjoy this book as much as I enjoyed putting it together. In fact, you can look at this as the inaugural volume in the **Living Room Art Gallery** series, as plans are already underway for future volumes featuring Angel artwork, Classical Female Figures, Classic Men, (clothed men), and many more to be announced. (They may already be available by the time you're reading this!). But for now, let's get started with this grand volume of classic art of the male figure, that is sure to bring beauty & wonder into your home!

Greg Fox
March, 2016

OPPOSITE PAGE:
TITLE: Standing Male Nude
ARTIST: Harold Knight
YEAR: 1896

A NOTE ABOUT ORIENTATION: The first 36 prints in this book are meant to be viewed/framed/hung vertically, ("portrait style")...and the final 13 prints are meant to be viewed/framed/hung horizontally, ("landscape style"). So, to view those last 13 prints in this book, simply rotate the book 90 degrees clockwise.

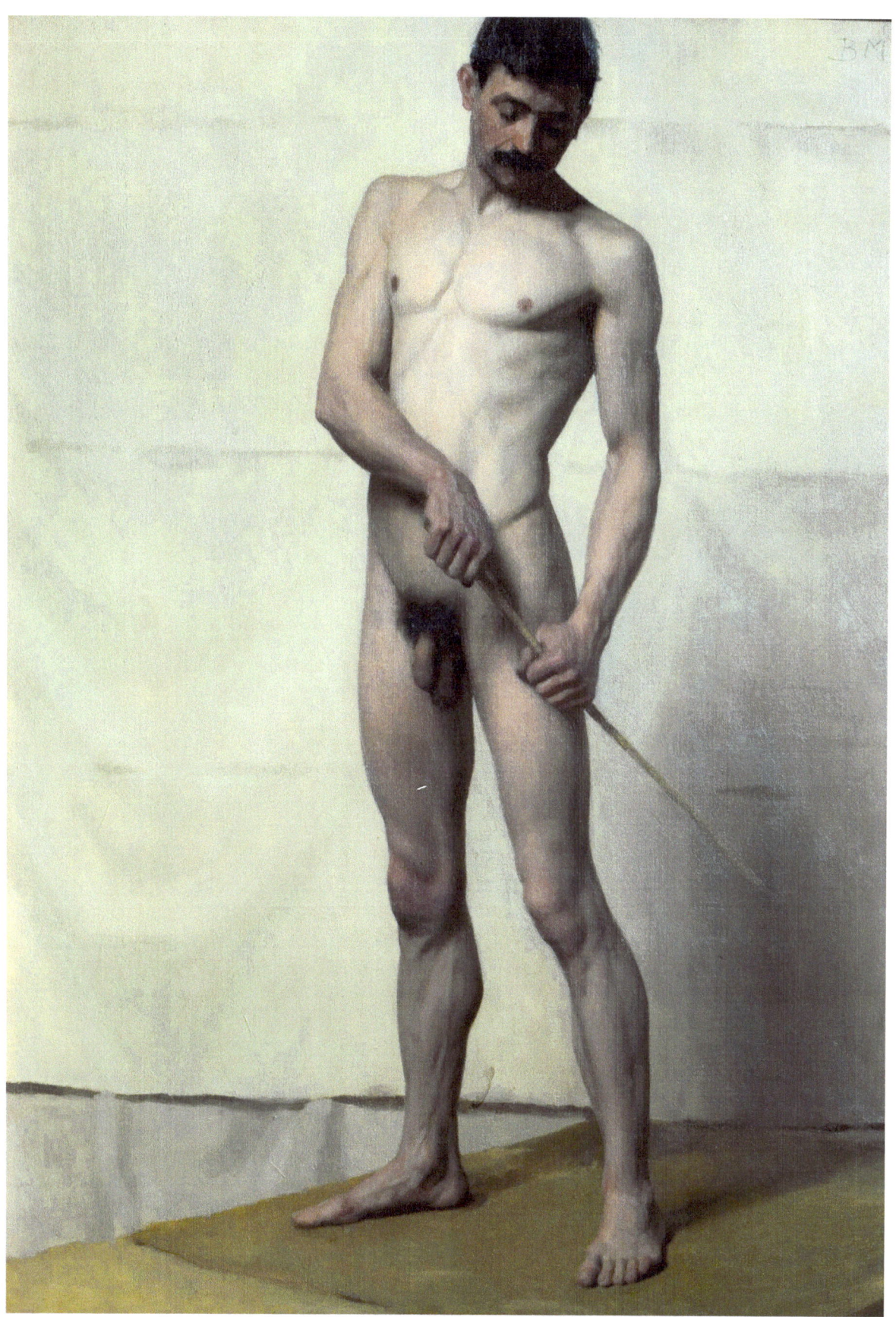

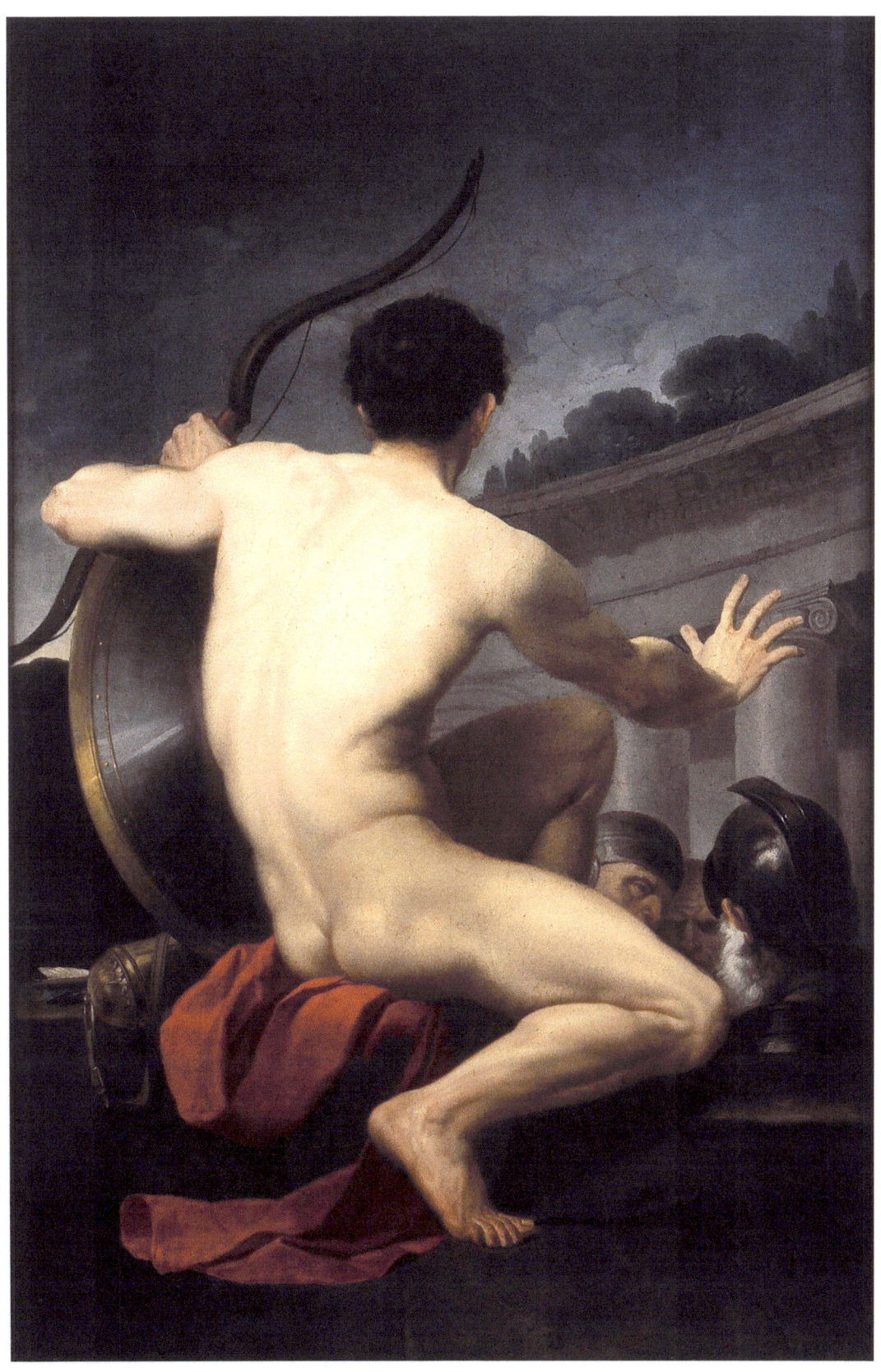

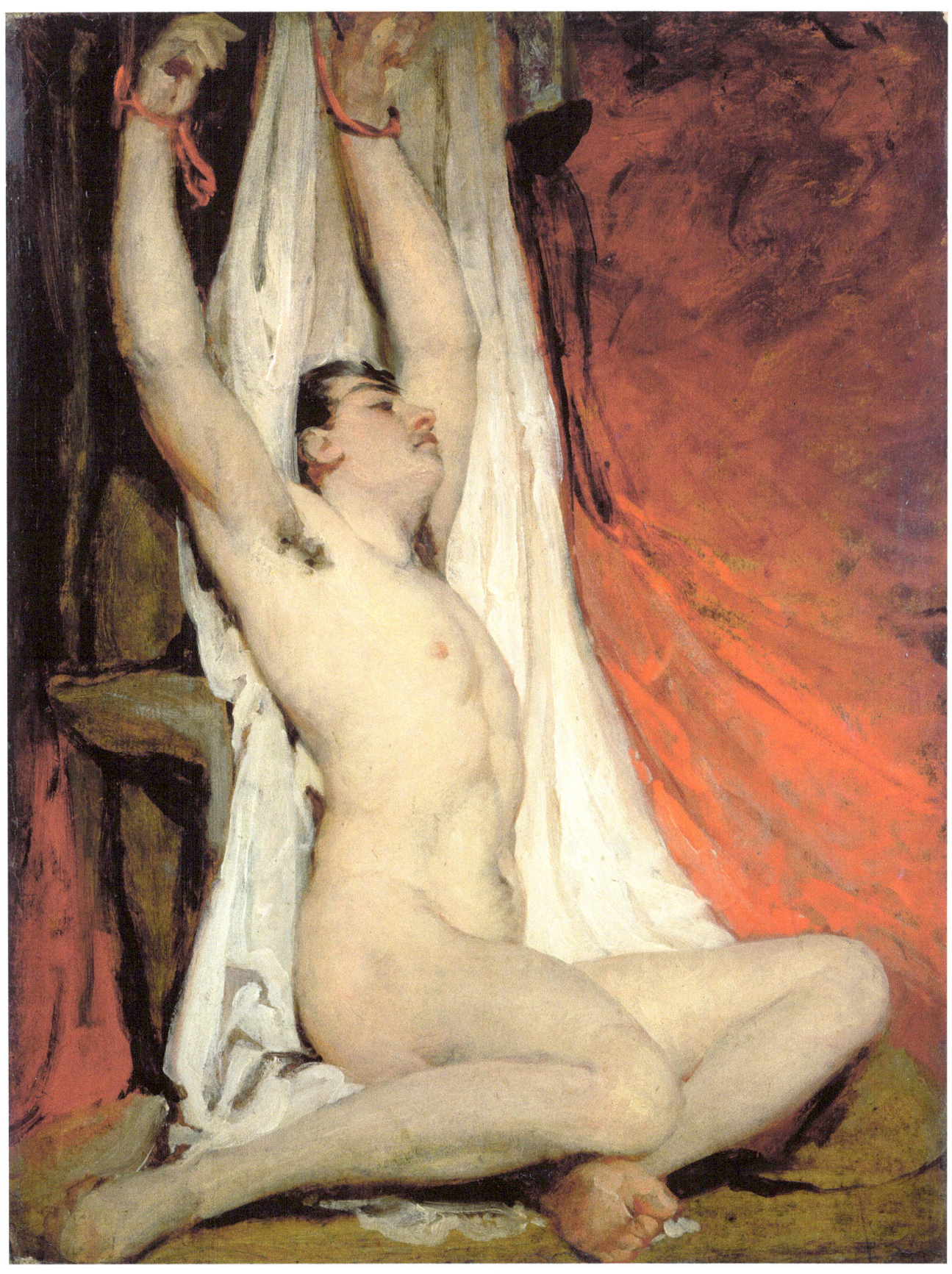

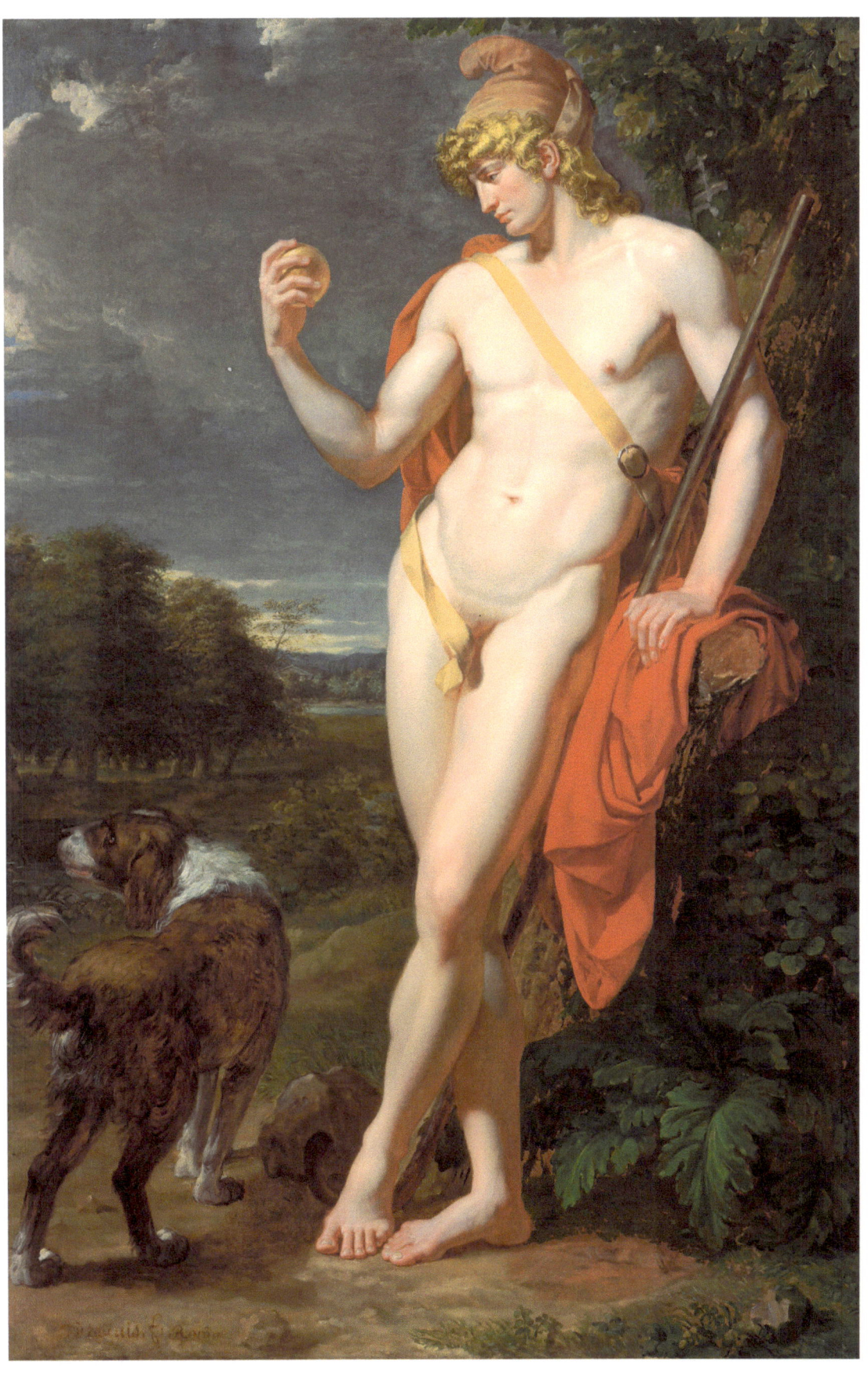

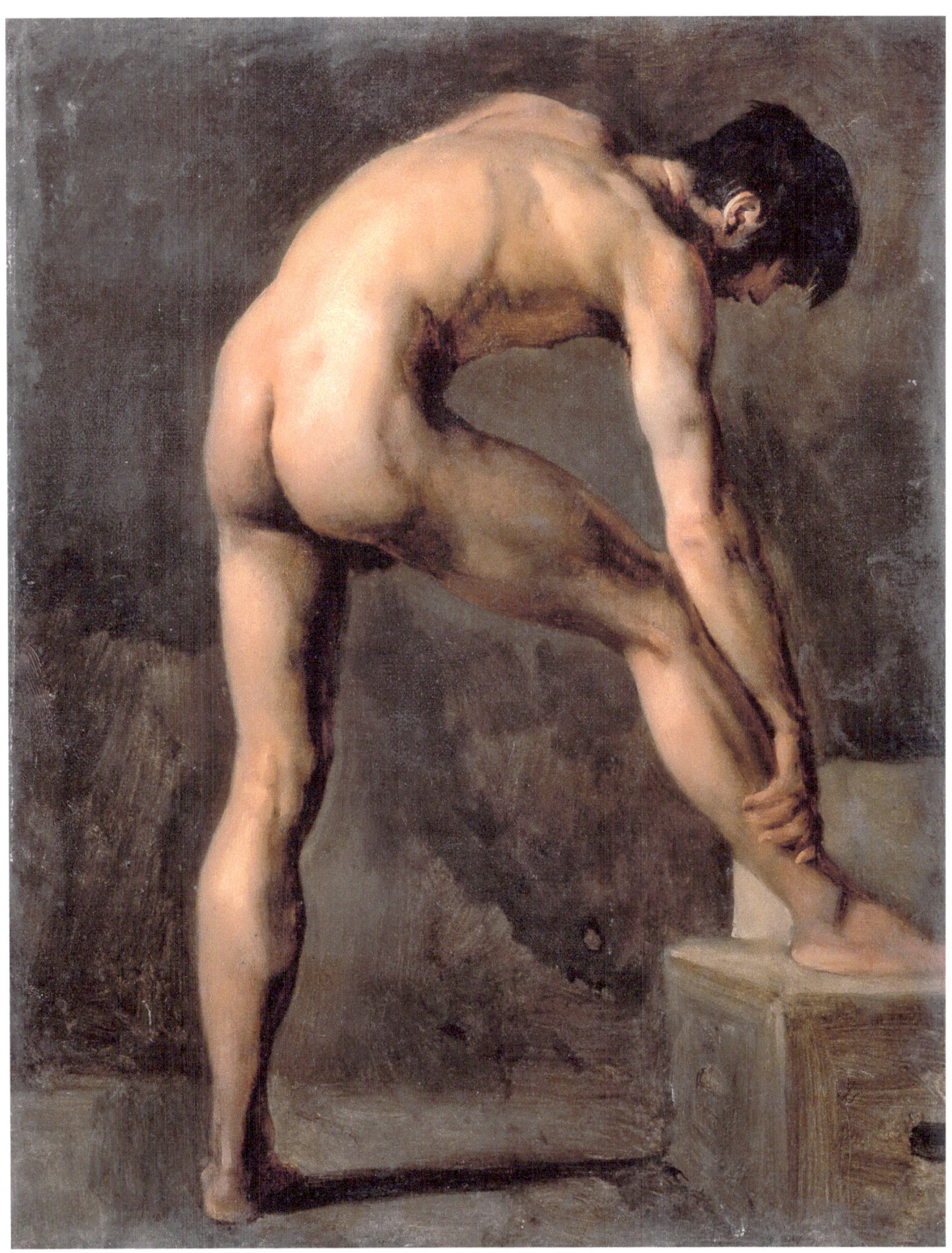

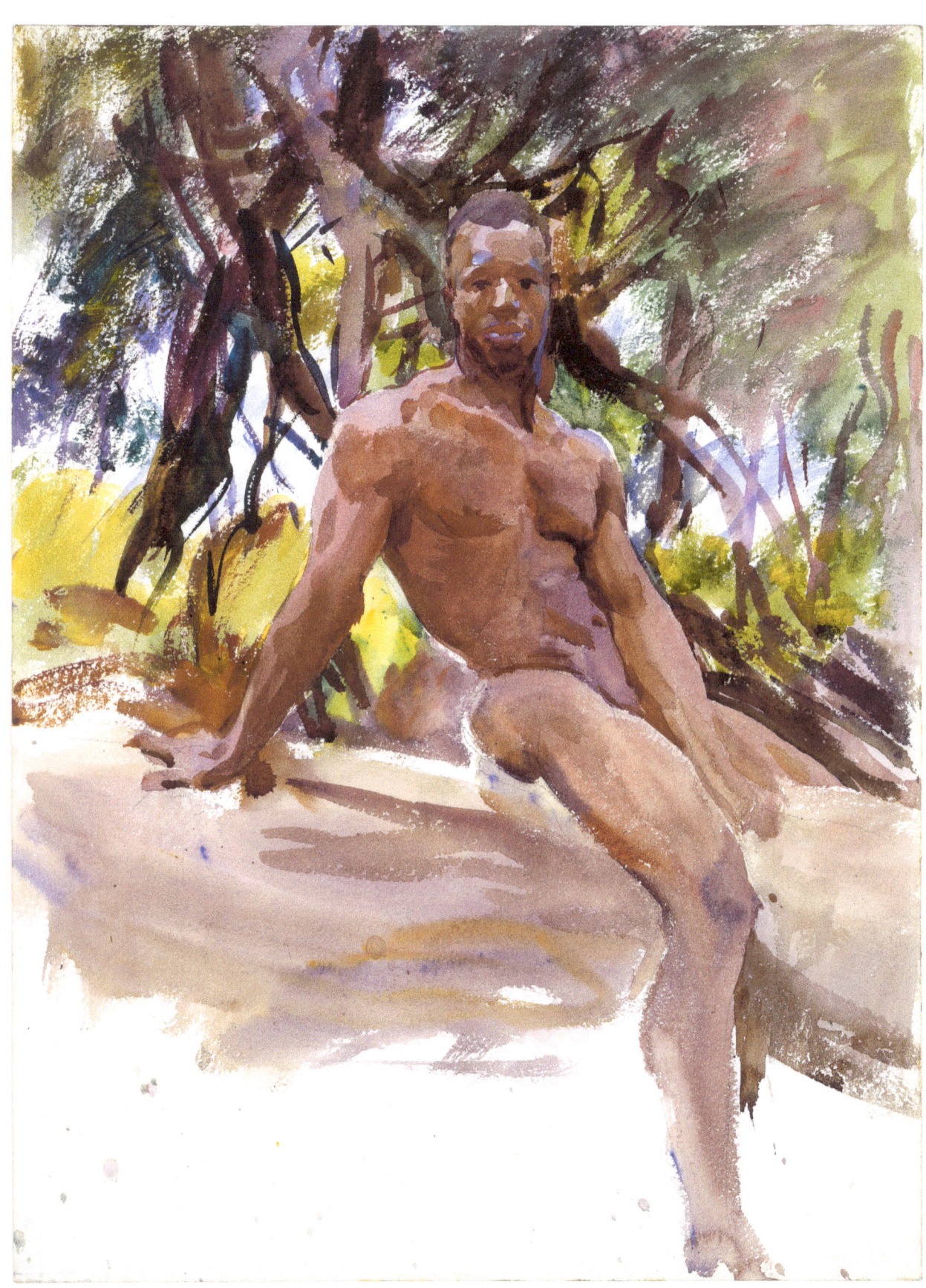

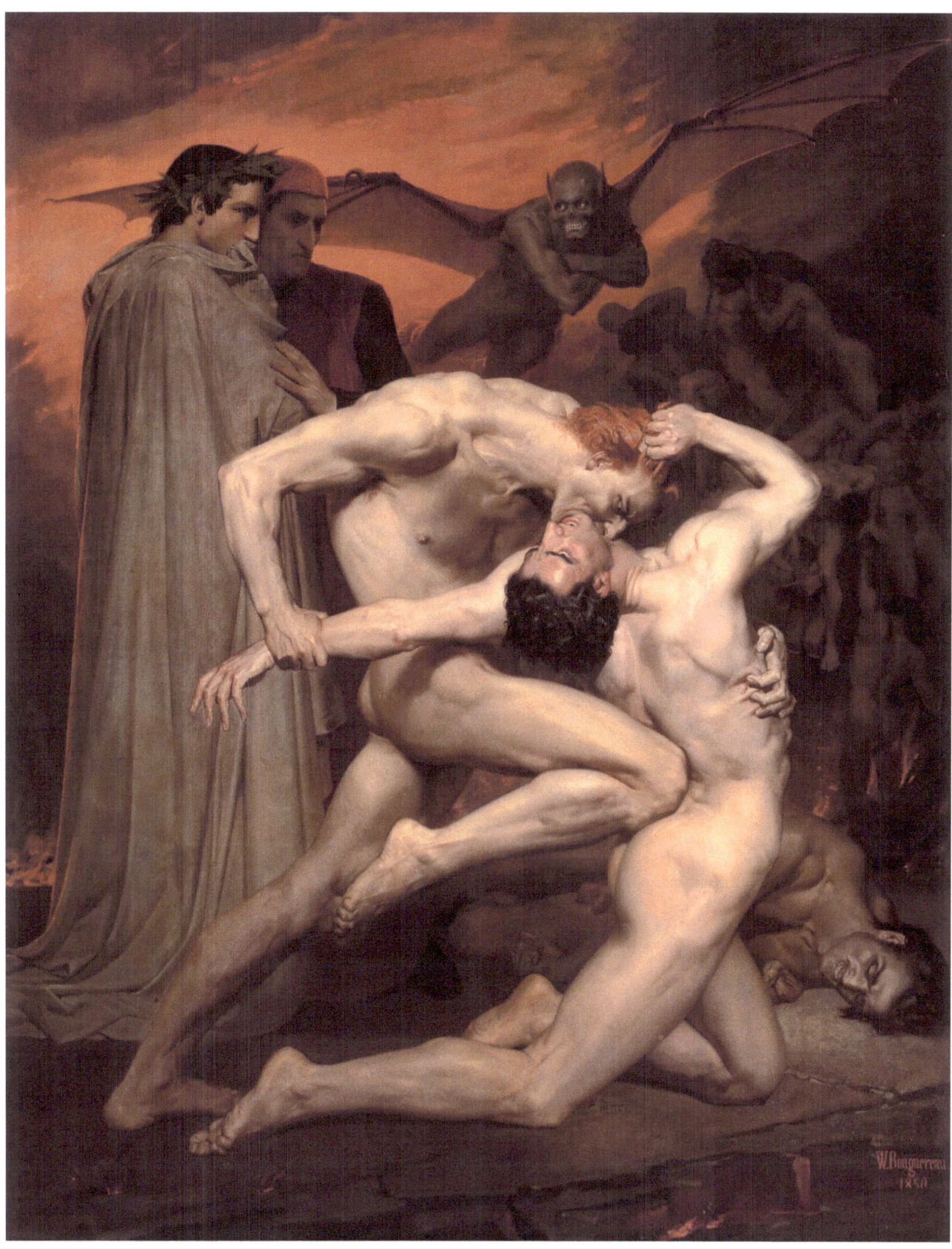

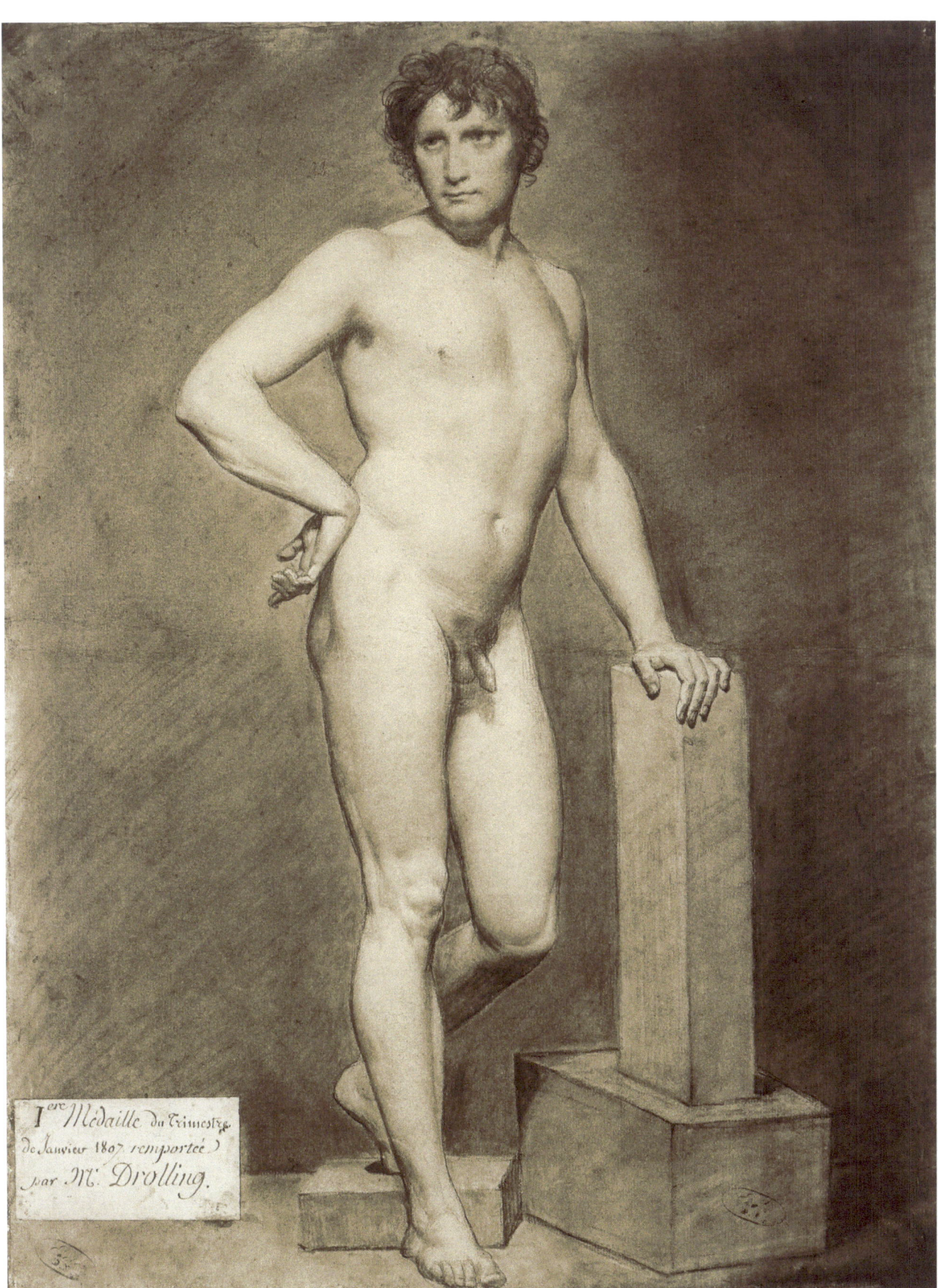

Iere Médaille du Trimestre de Janvier 1807 remportée par Mr. Drolling.

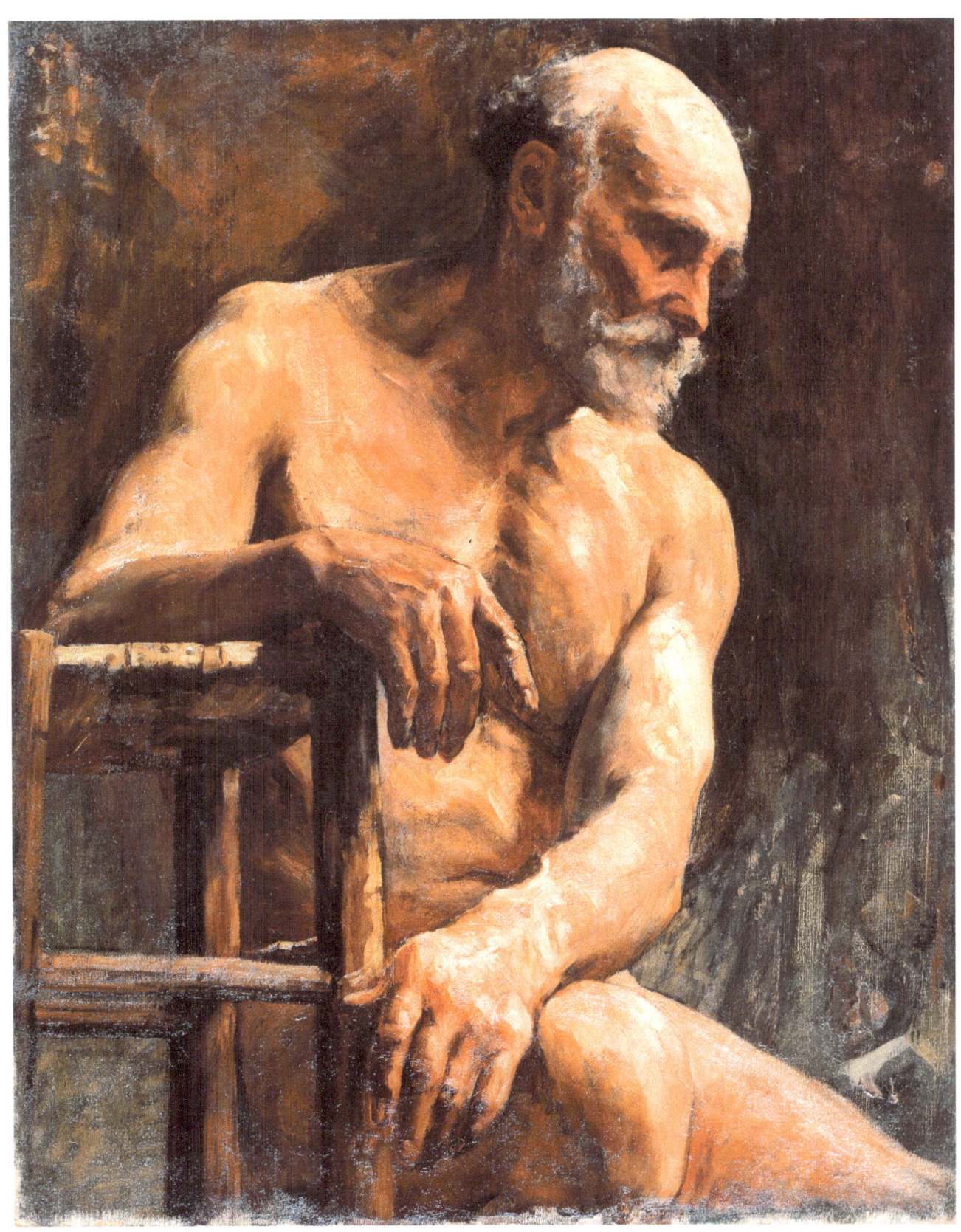

OPPOSITE PAGE:
TITLE: Charon Ferrying the Shades
ARTIST: Pierre Subleyras
YEAR: between 1735 and 1740

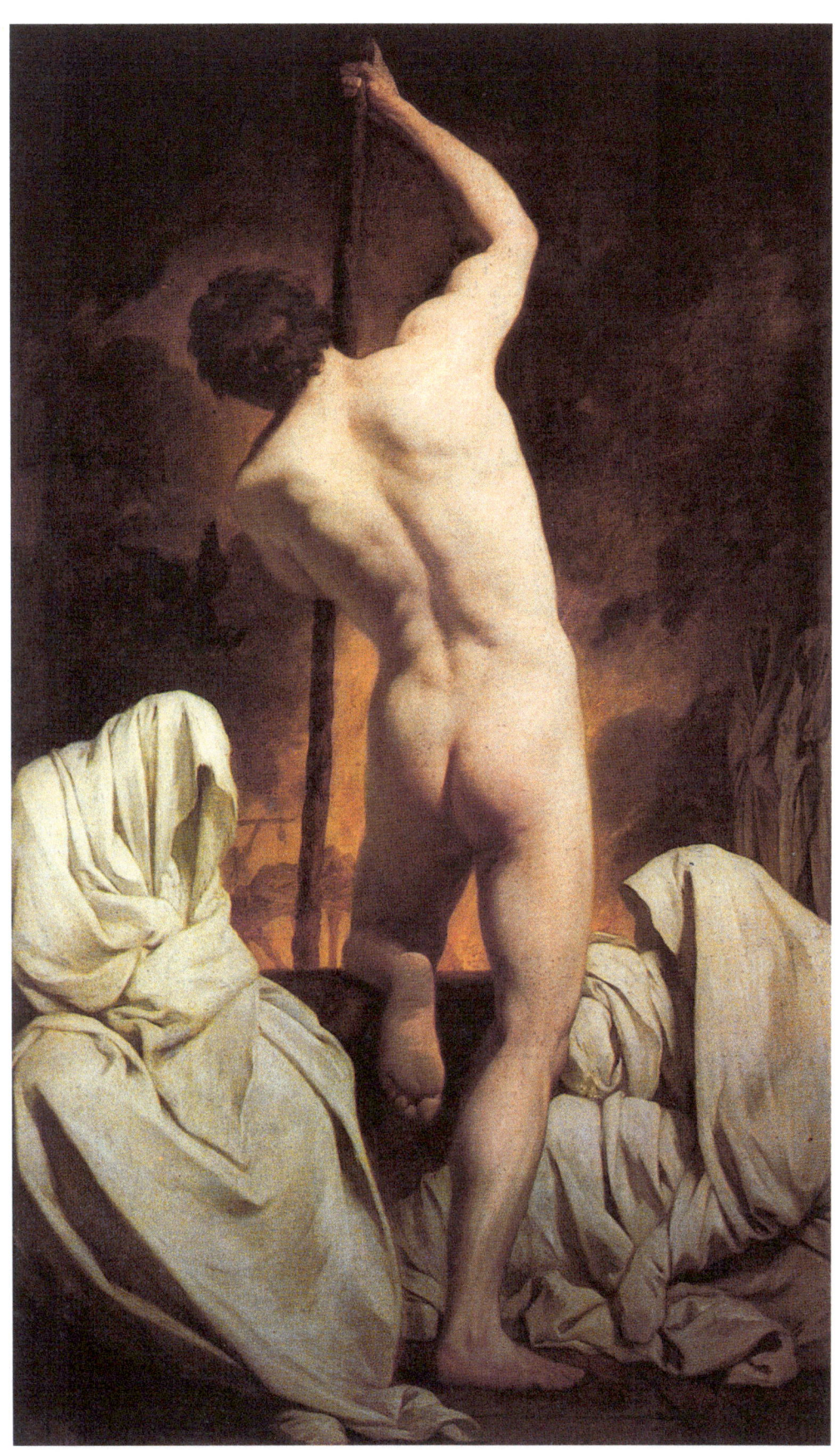

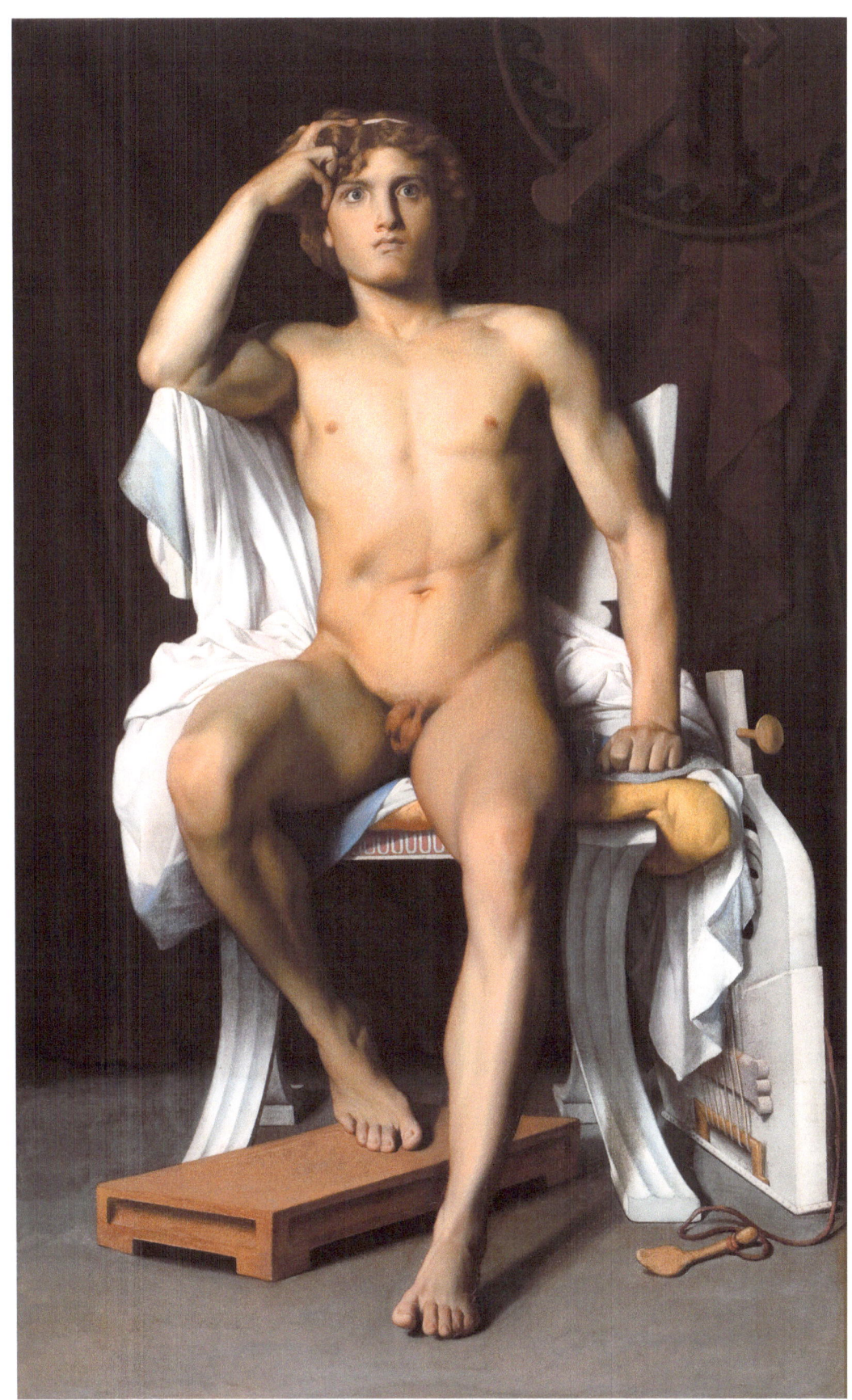

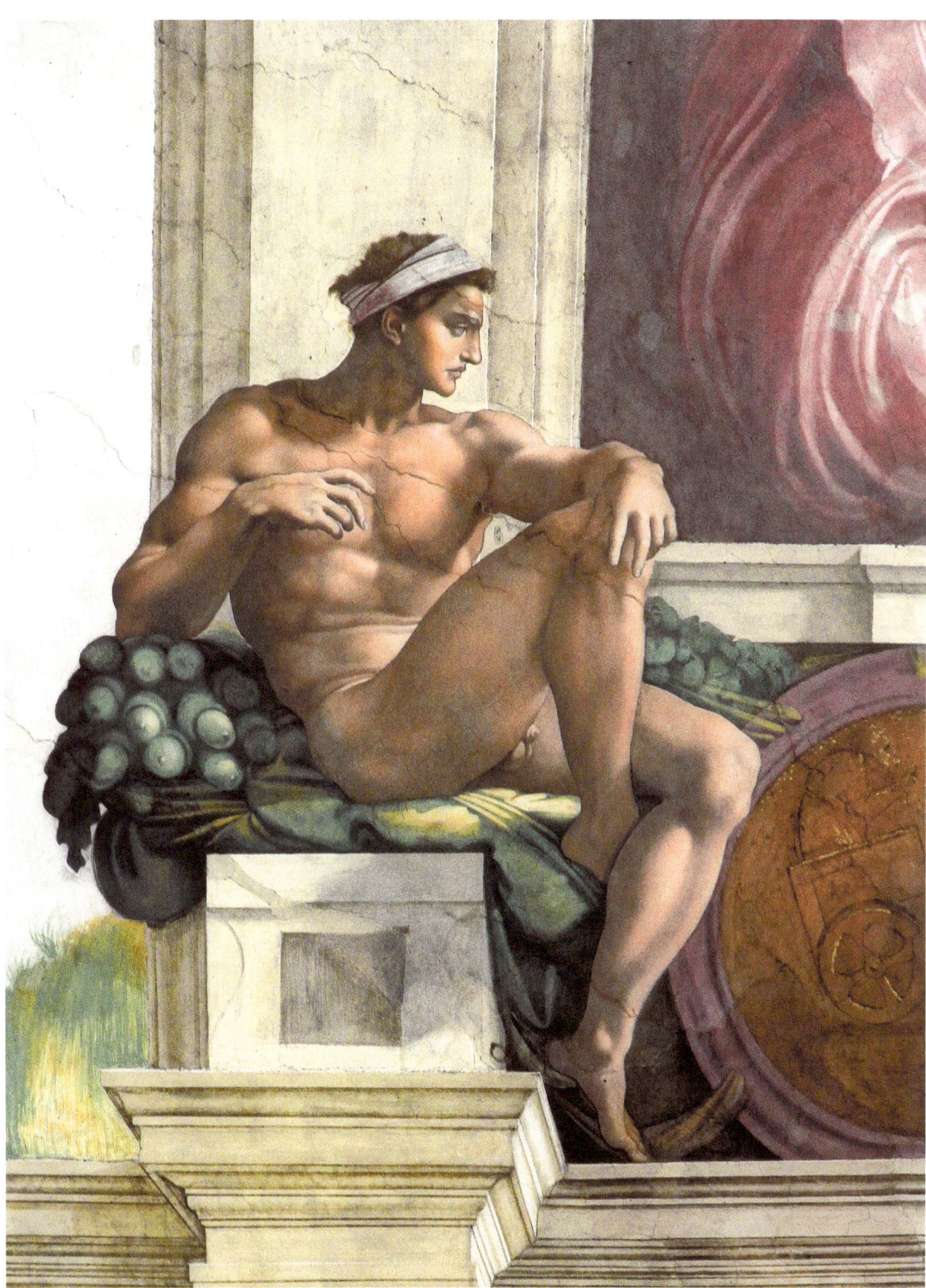

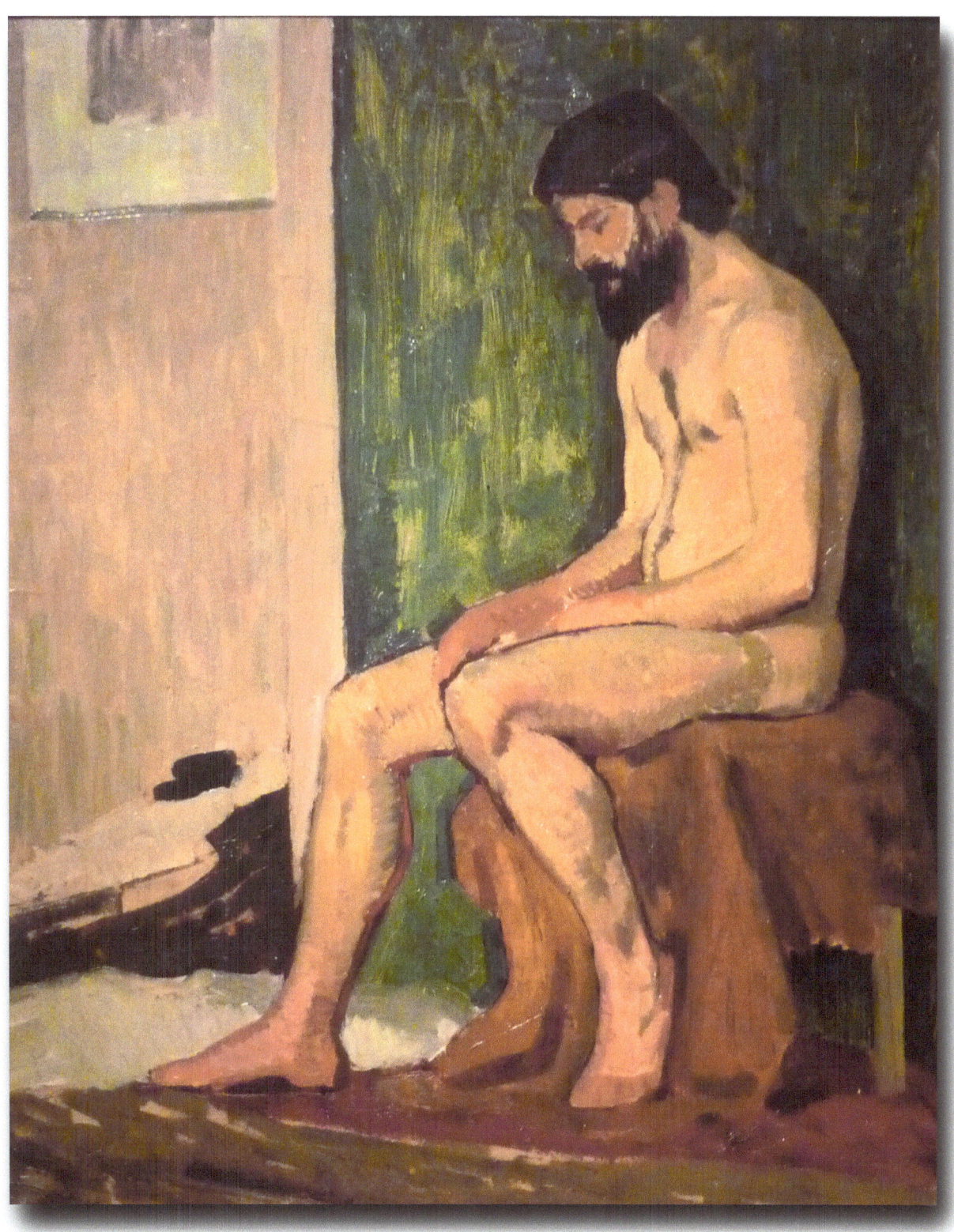

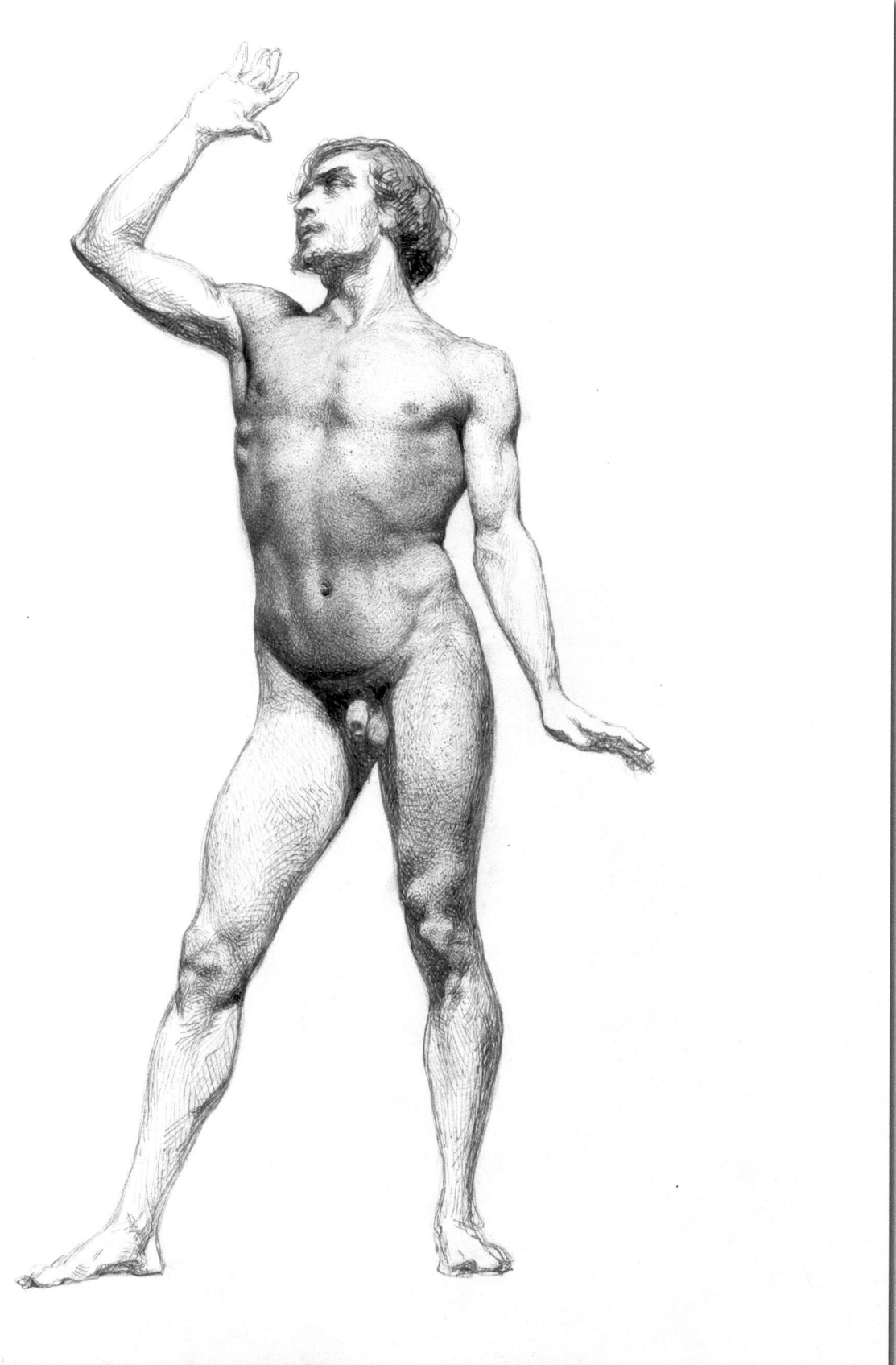

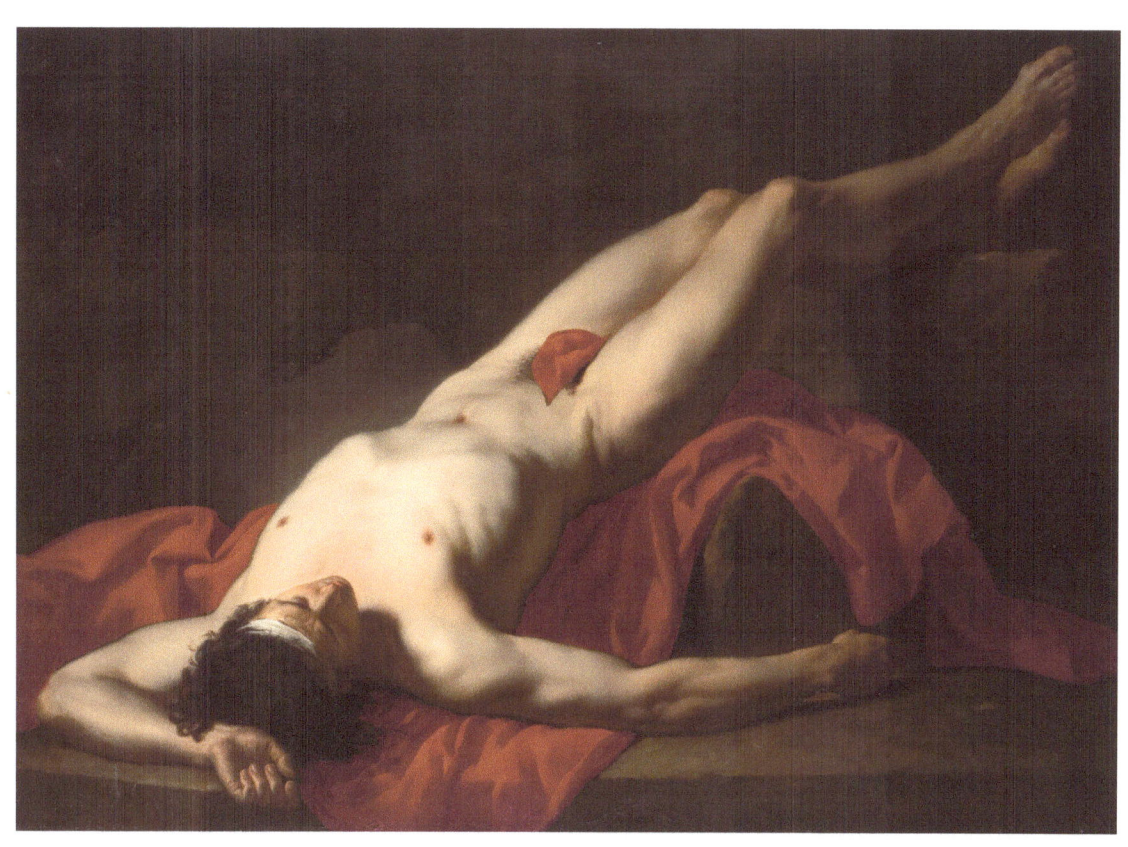

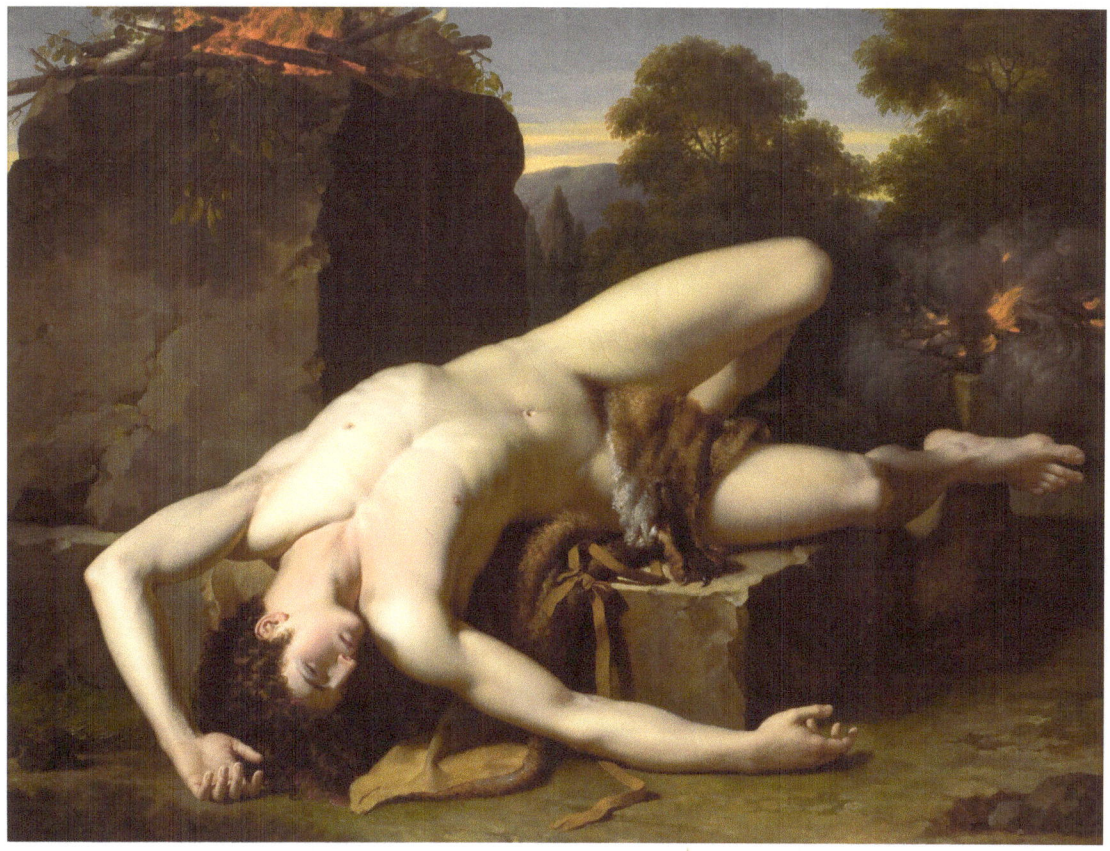

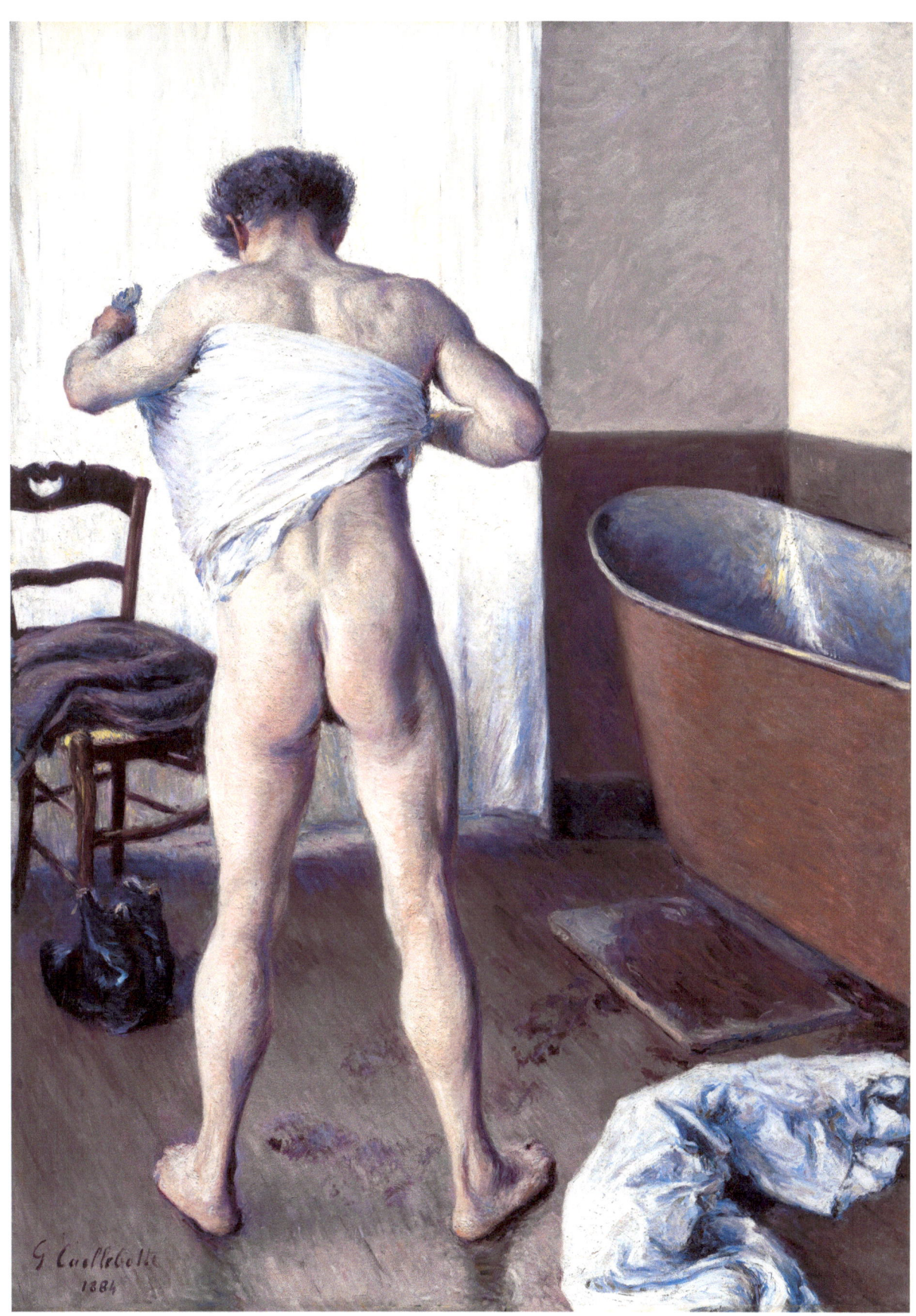

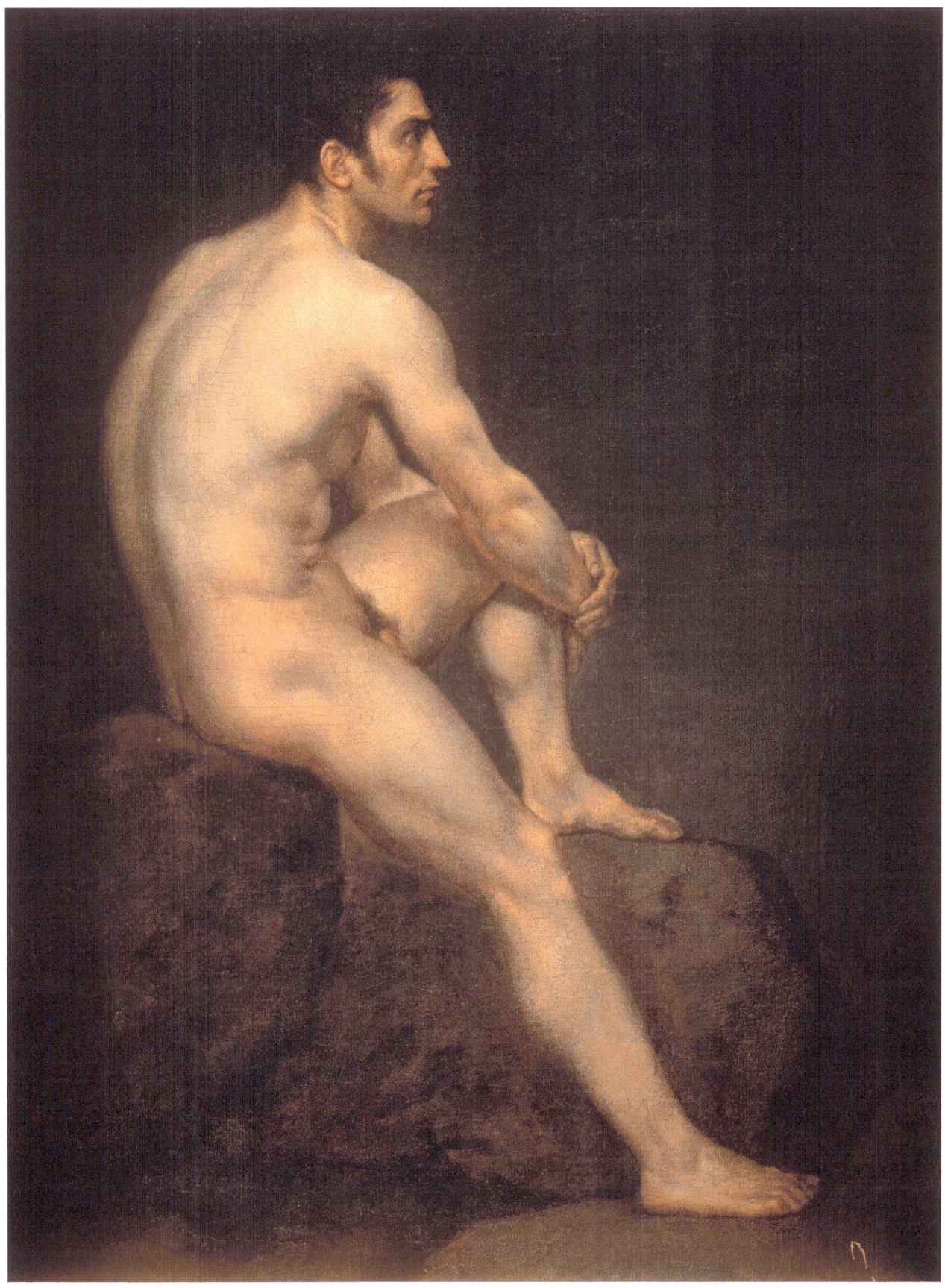

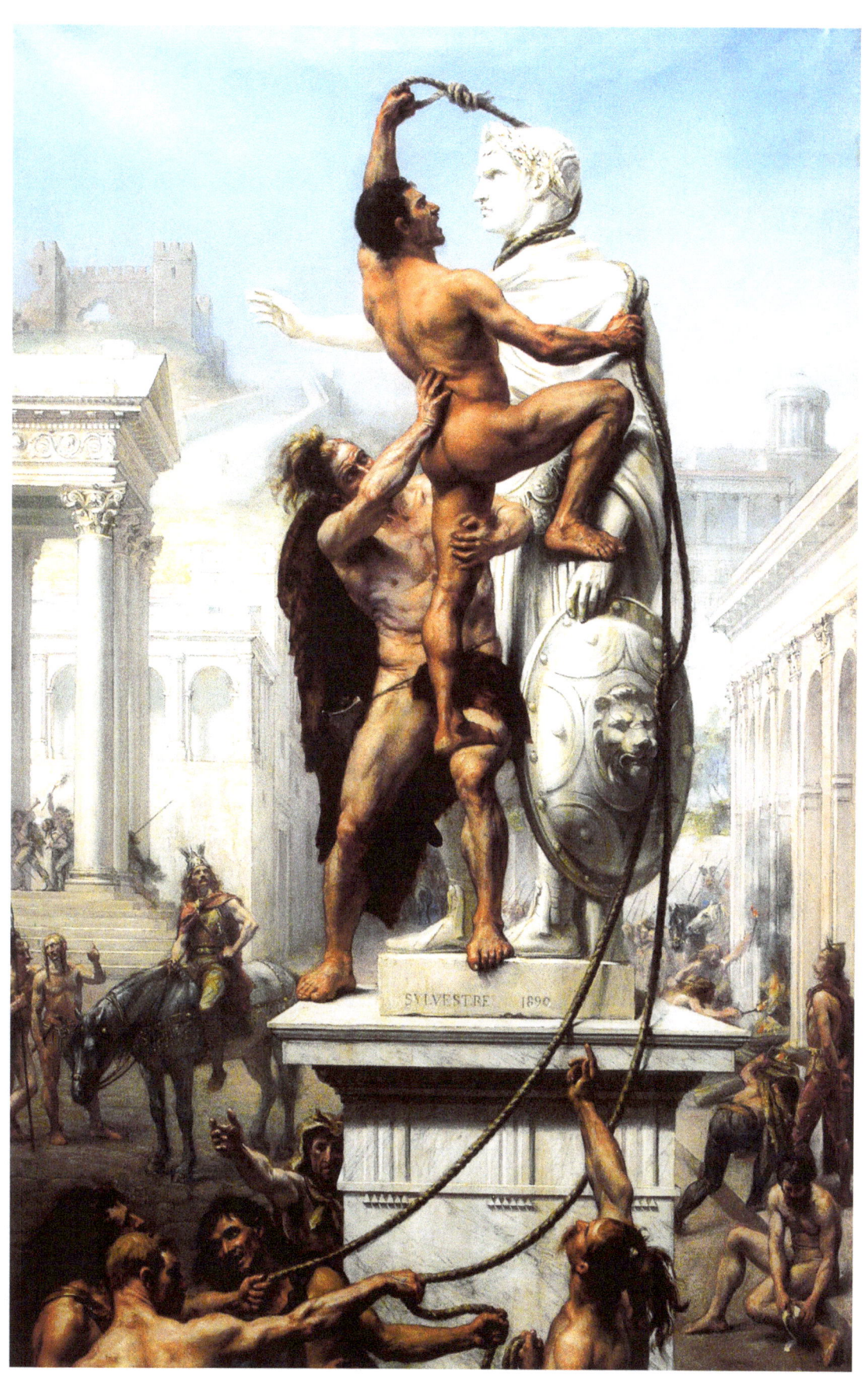

SYLVESTRE 1890

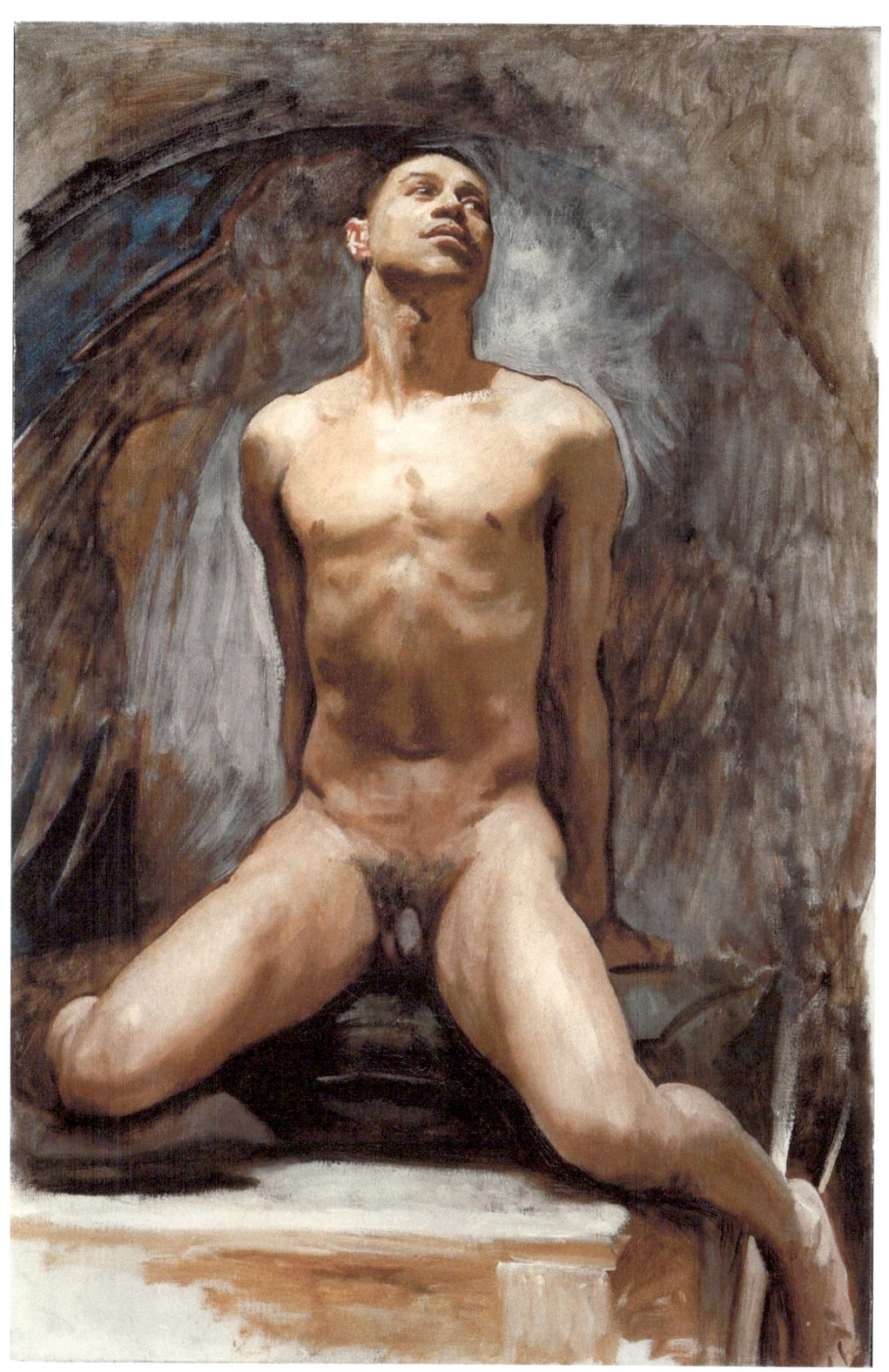

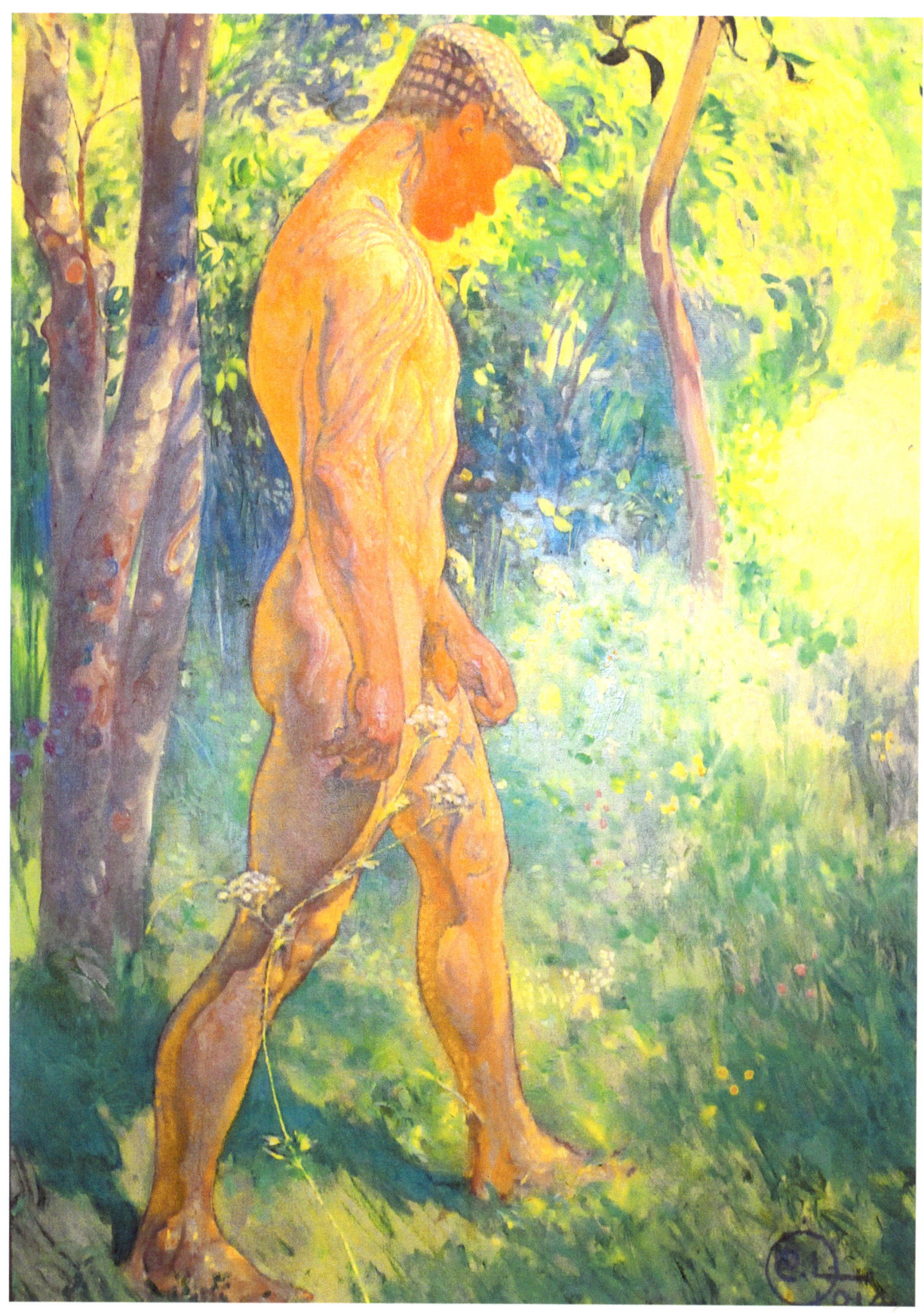

Who doesn't love a good mystery? When this painting was originally posted to the Classical Male Figure Page on Facebook, the source I got it from listed Jacques-Louis David as the artist, and the year of creation as 1835. Right off the bat, that was a problem, as Jacques-Louis David *died* in **1825**! And frankly, it looked a lot more to me like the work of Jean-Auguste-Dominique Ingres, another French painter, (who studied under Jacques-Louis David earlier in his career, and who also happened to still be *alive* in 1835!). The matter was hardly settled, though, as I could not find any confirmation of this fact in several books on Ingres, and nowhere online, either, (and believe me... I looked!). What I did find, however, was the image to the left... an academic study of a male nude by Ingres from 1801, in which the model and pose look strikingly similar to the one on the opposite page, (albeit at a different viewing angle), right down to the hanging white drapery. Which pointed to the possibility that both paintings were done by Ingres during his time studying in the studio of Jacques-Louis David. Which would also mean that the date of 1835 is wrong, and 1801 would be correct, (and also means Jacques-Louis David would've been alive at that time, further muddling the issue on whether or not *he* painted it!). What to do?

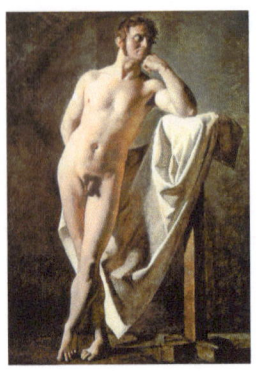

It looked to me like I had three options:

1. Hold off on publishing this book until I got 100 percent confirmation on who the artist is, (not really an option, as I'd already spent too much time researching this, and it did not look like any sort of clarification would be forthcoming at any time soon, if ever).
2. Don't include this painting in the book, (something I also didn't want to do, as the more time I spent researching this, the more I really grew to like this painting, and wanted it to be part of this book).
3. Include the painting, and also include this somewhat long-winded explanation of the mystery behind it.

As you can see, I chose option # 3. I do not think this painting should fall into the shadows and be denied to the world because of the mystery of its creator, (who I do strongly believe is Jean-Auguste-Dominique Ingres). And I also realized that by including it here, and detailing the mystery behind it, perhaps some Ingres/David expert will see it and come forward to verify once and for all just who the artist actually is! If you happen to be that expert, feel free to e-mail me at gregfox727@gmail.com

By the way, there is an Ingres painting on page 81 of this book, and two David paintings, on pages 35 and 61 of this book, if you're interested in comparing their styles. But, for now...enjoy this painting!!!

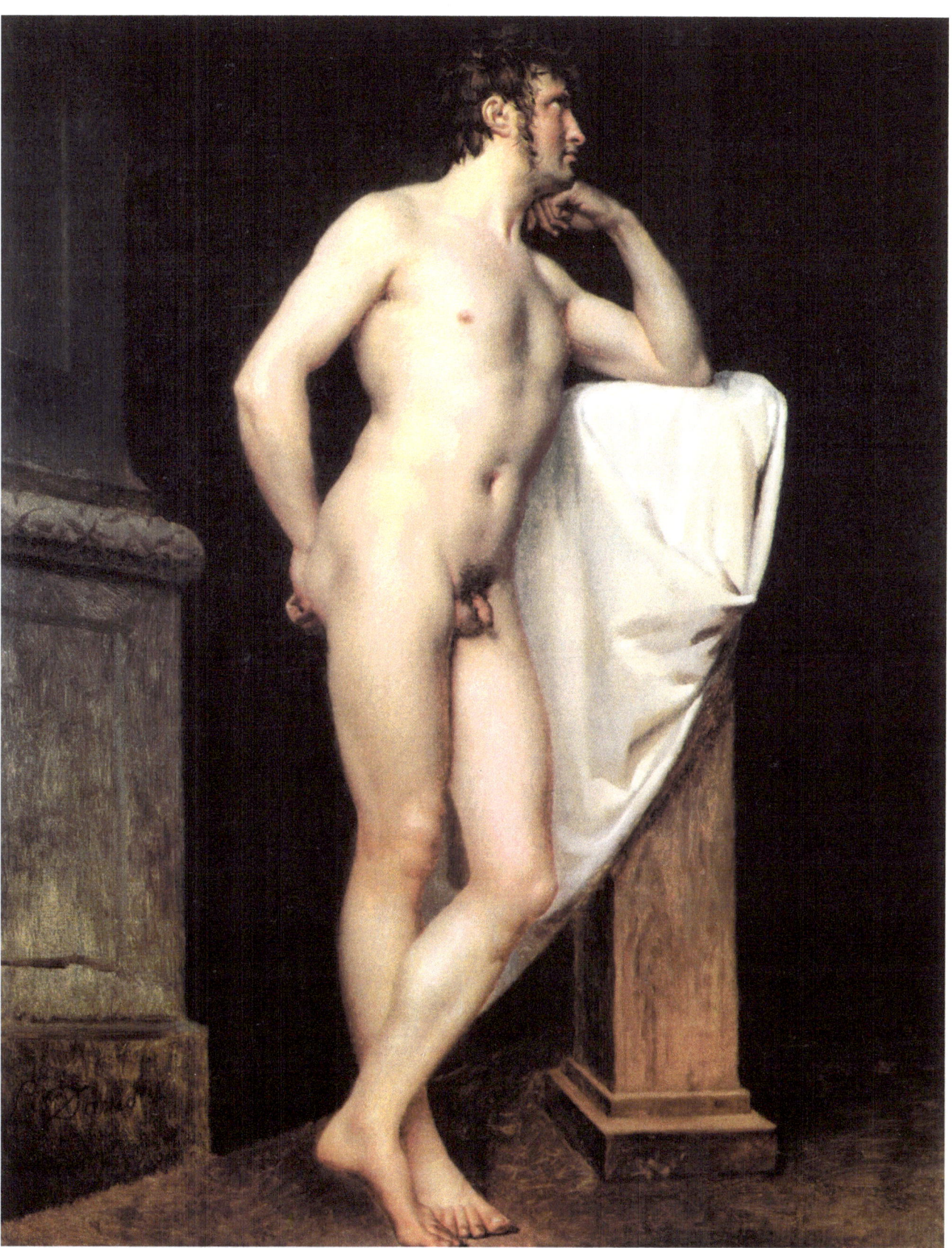

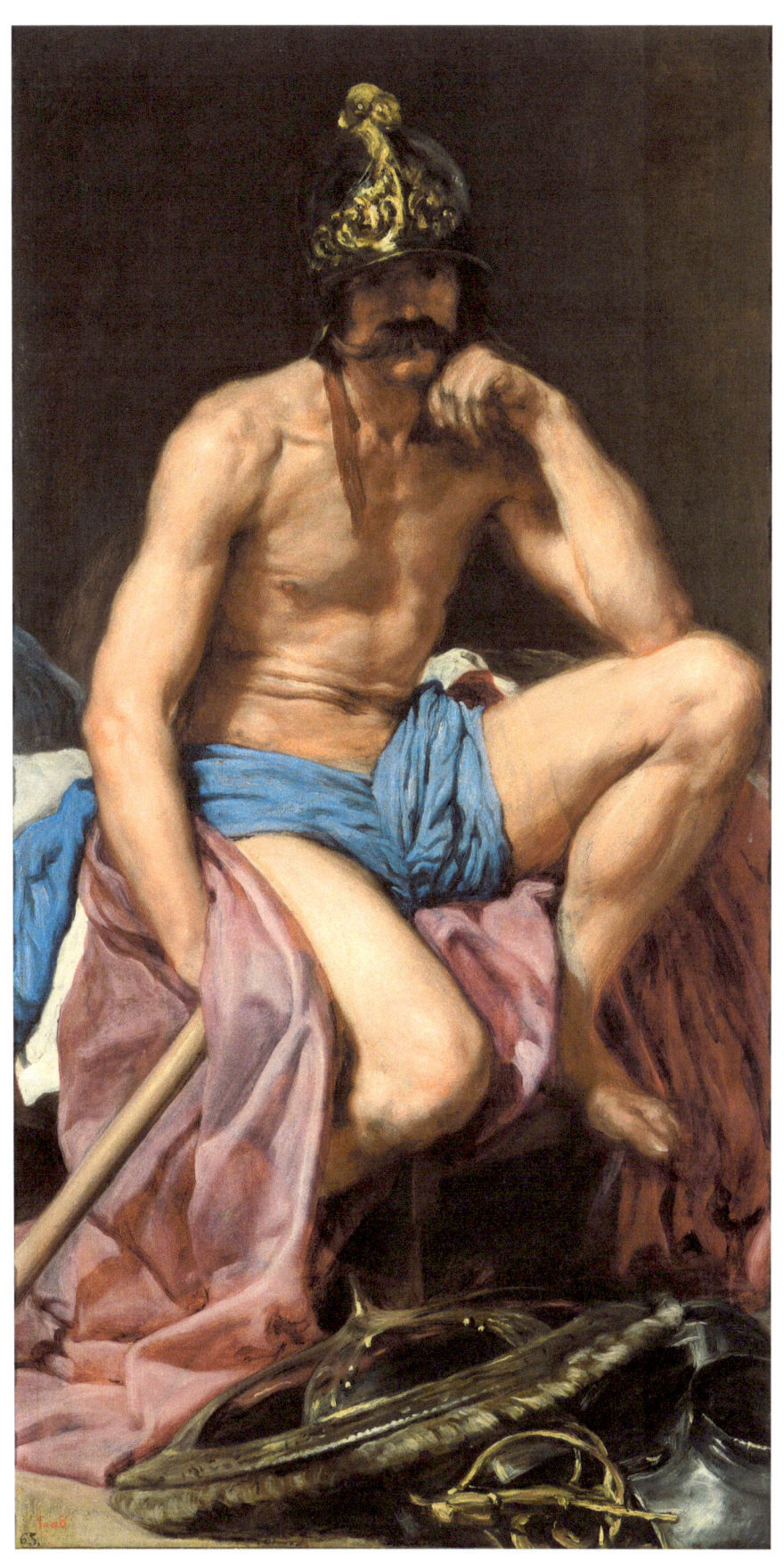

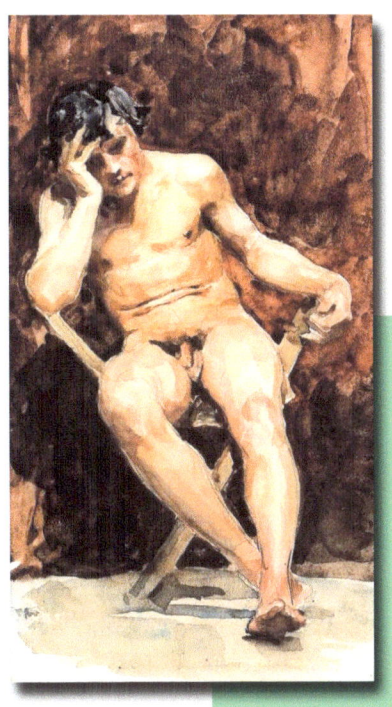
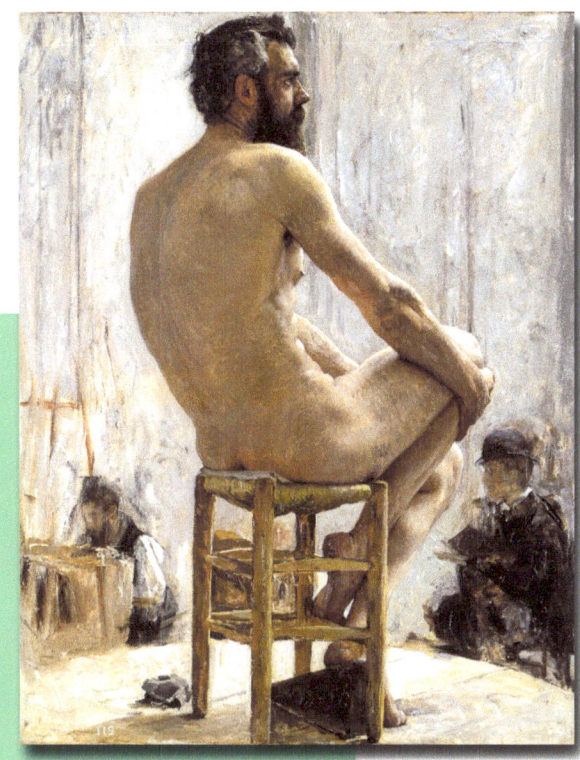
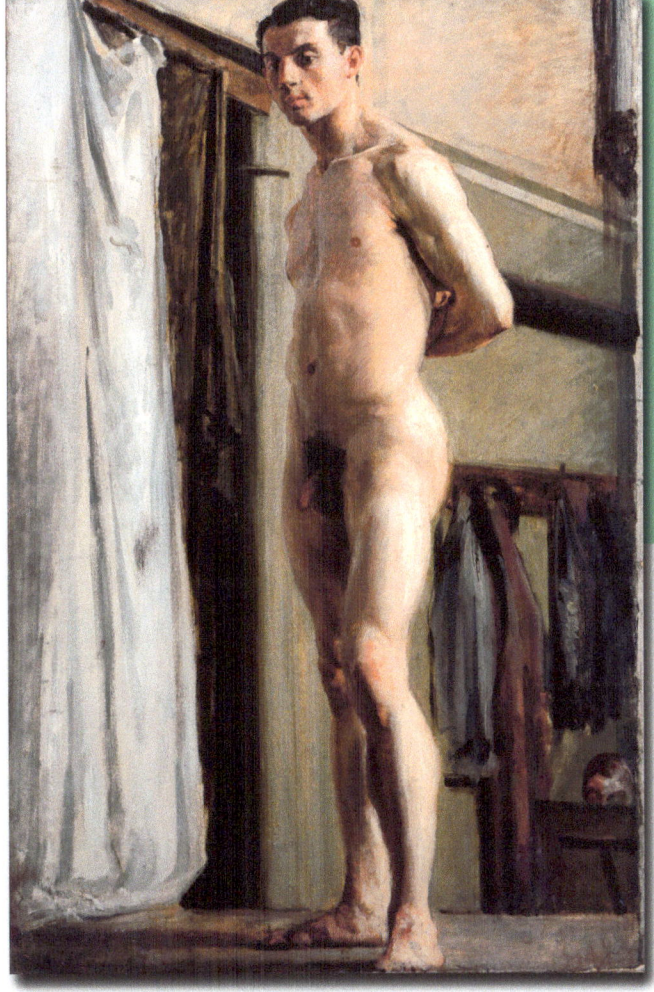
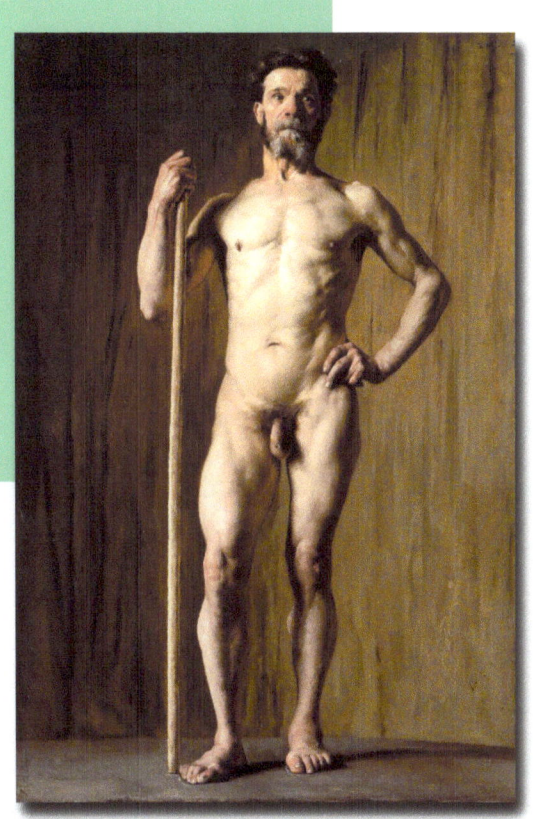

OPPOSITE PAGE:
TITLE: A Reading From Homer, (detail)
ARTIST: Sir Lawrence Alma-Tadema
YEAR: 1885

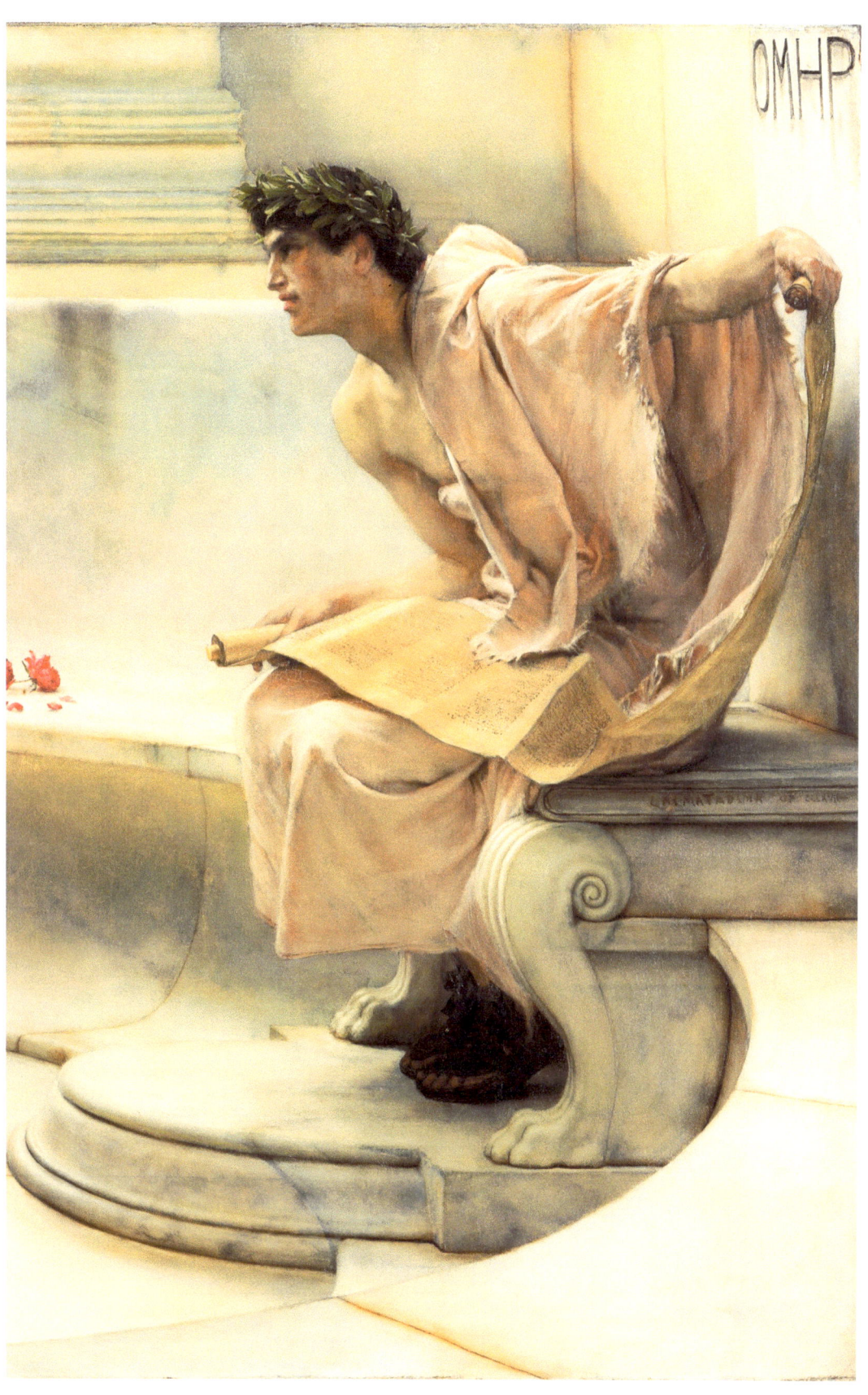

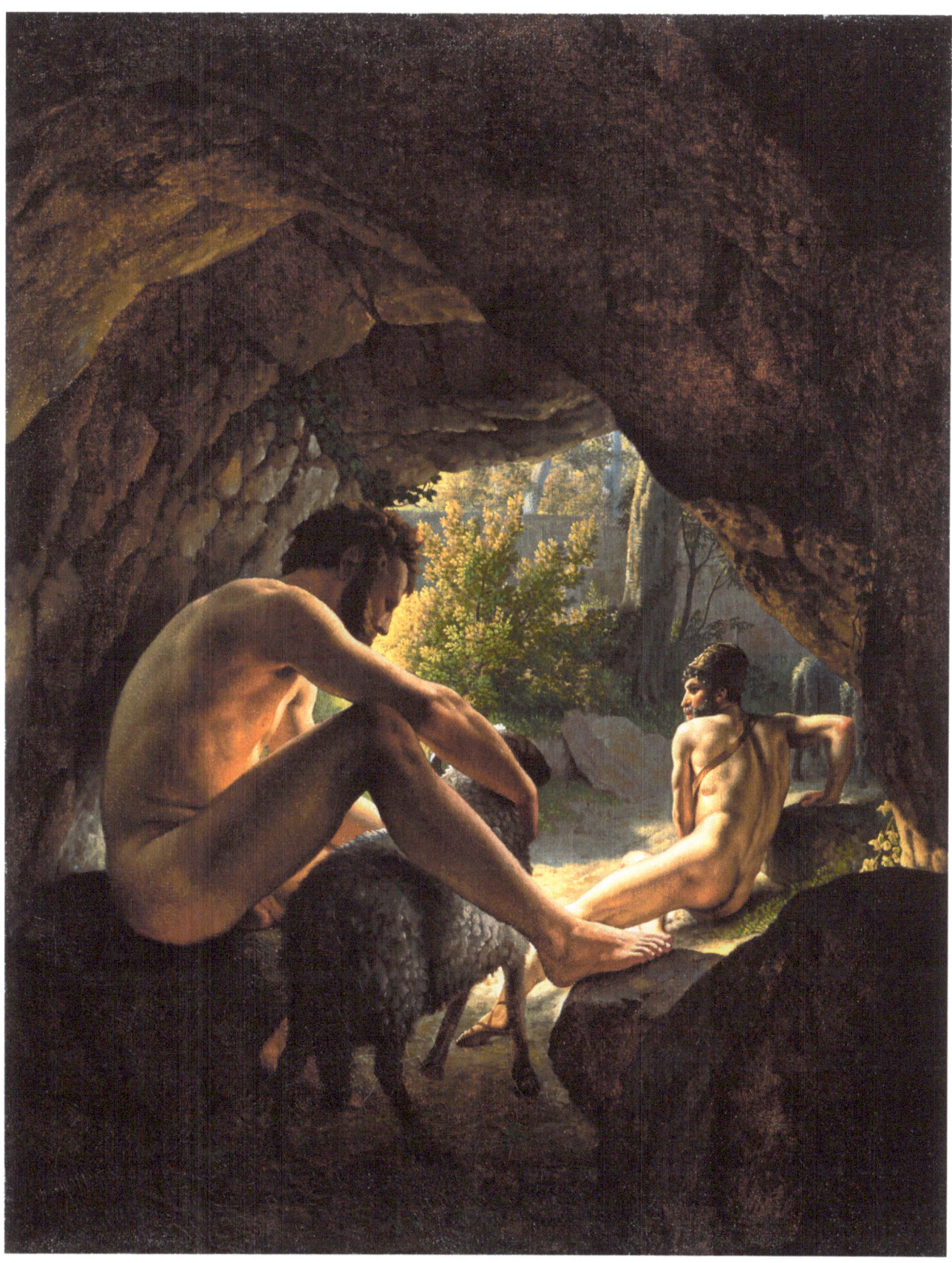

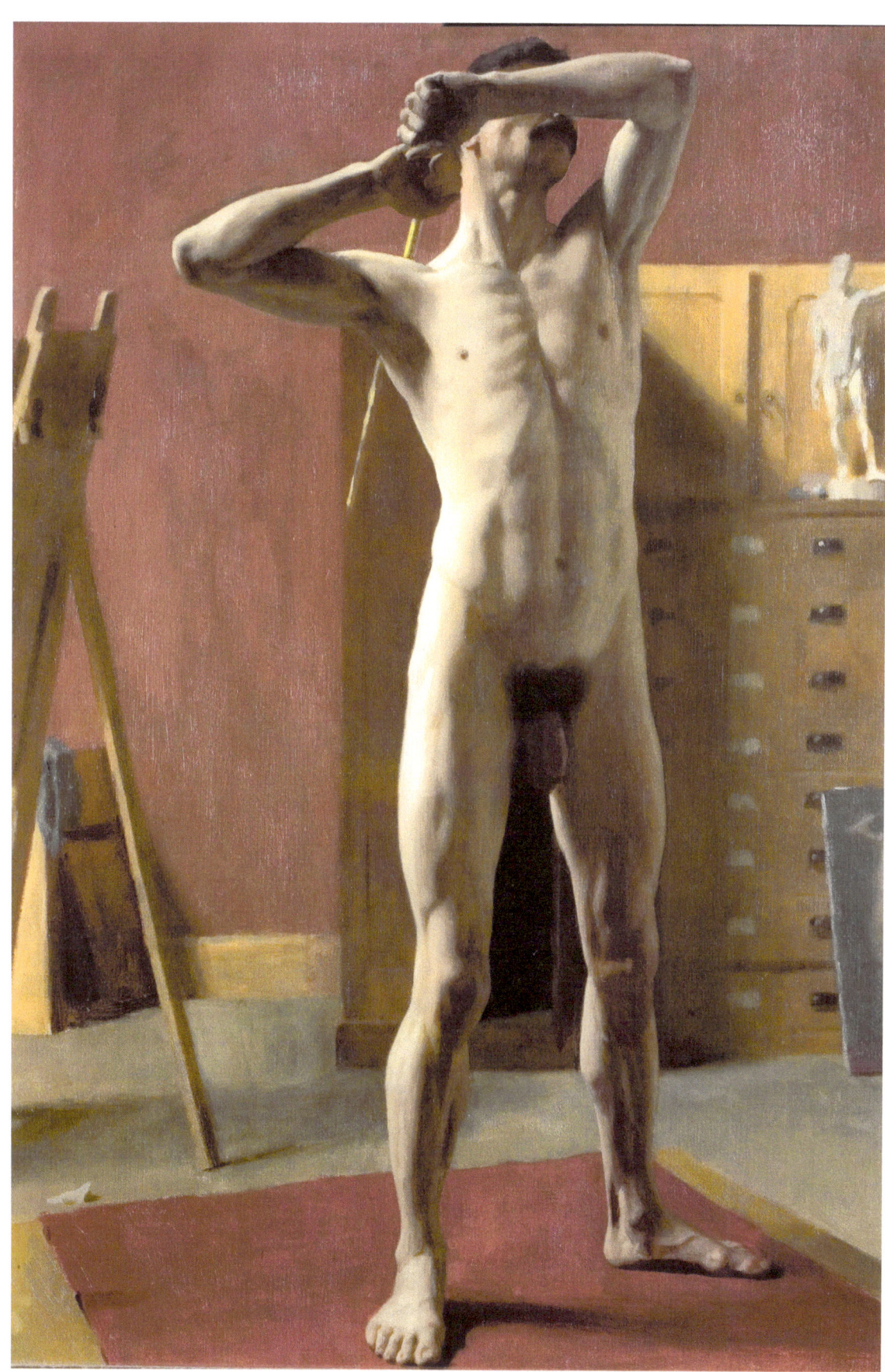

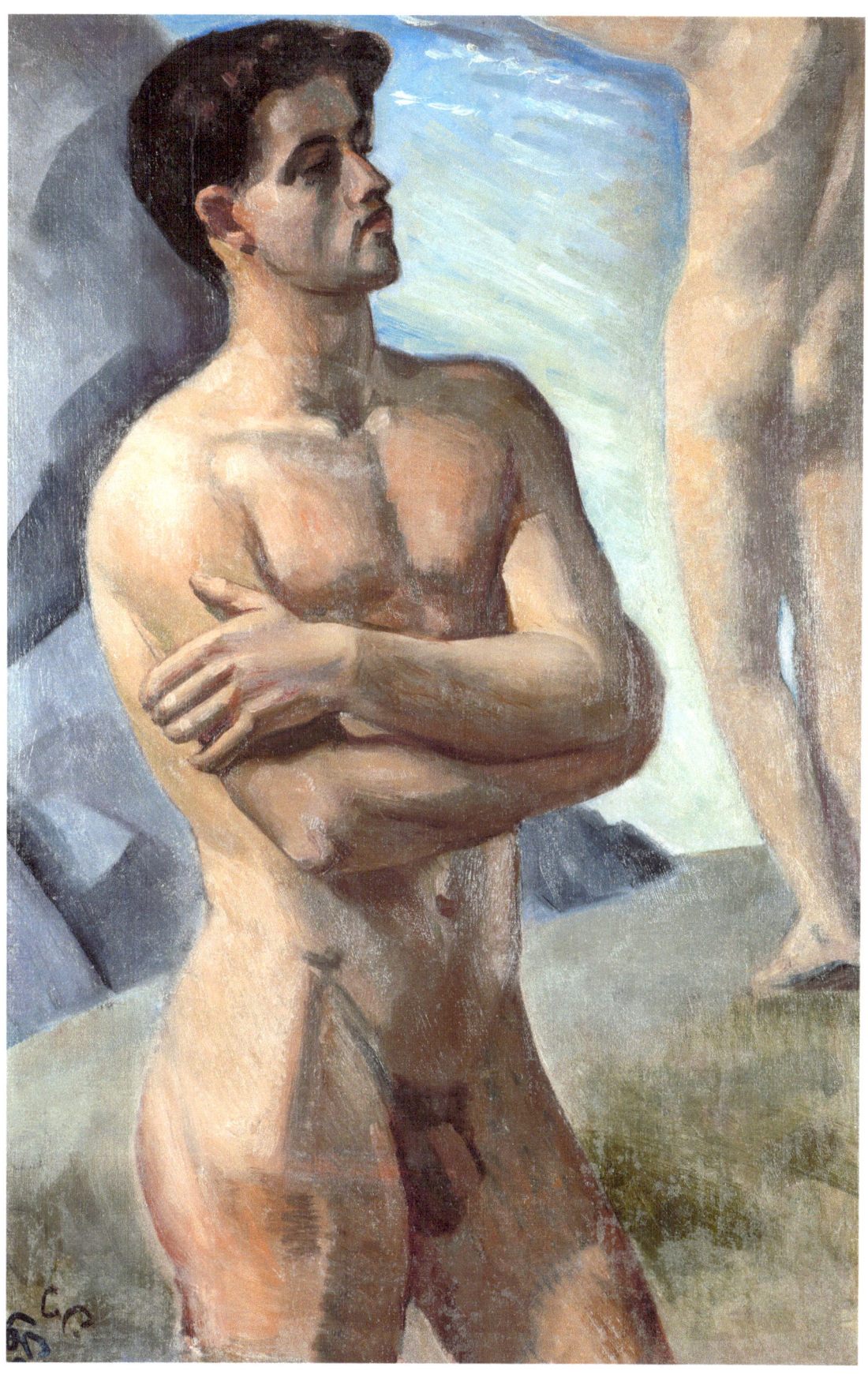

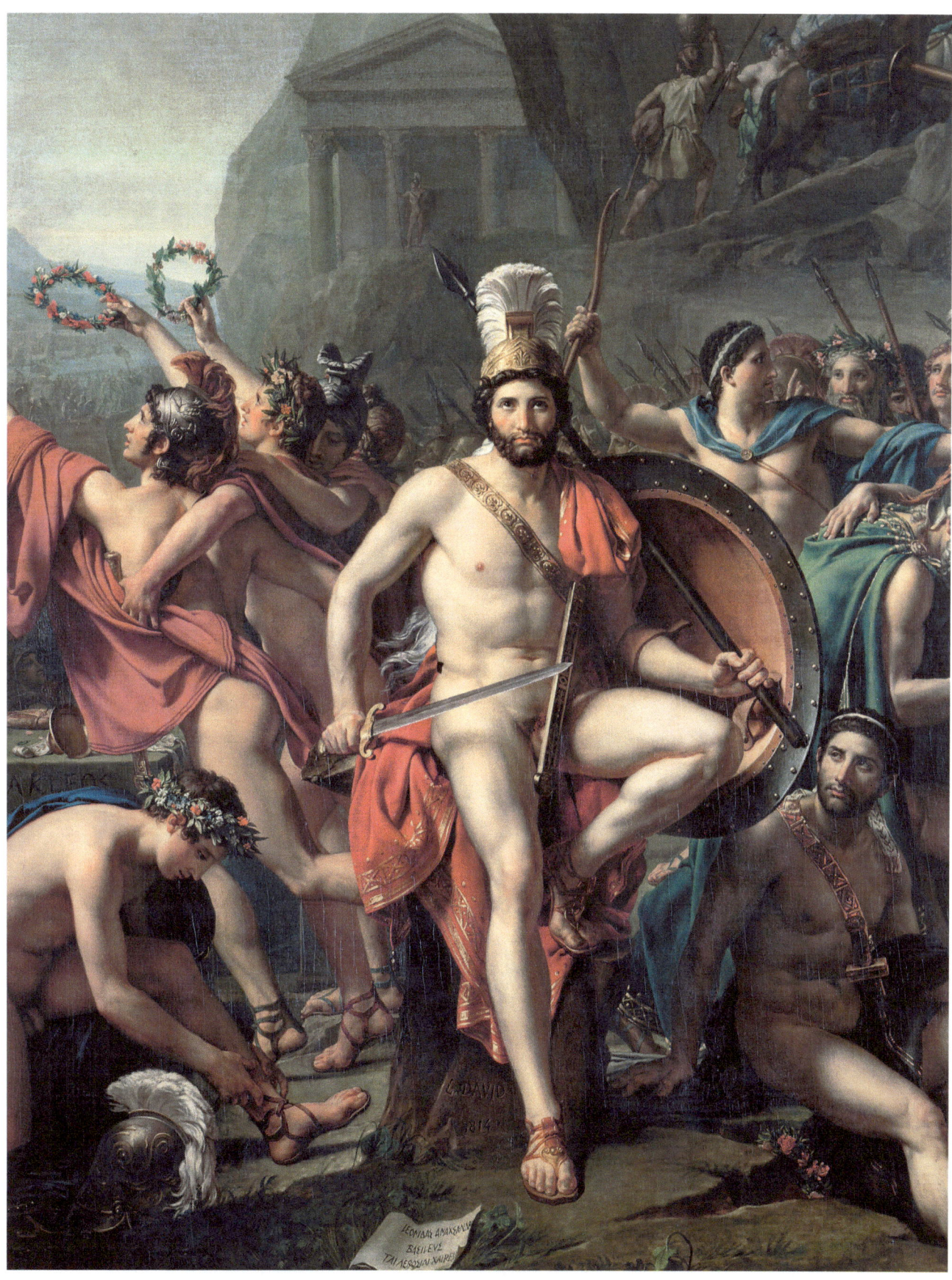

OPPOSITE PAGE:
TITLE: Seated Nude on White Chair
ARTIST: Eugène Jansson
YEAR: between 1906-1914

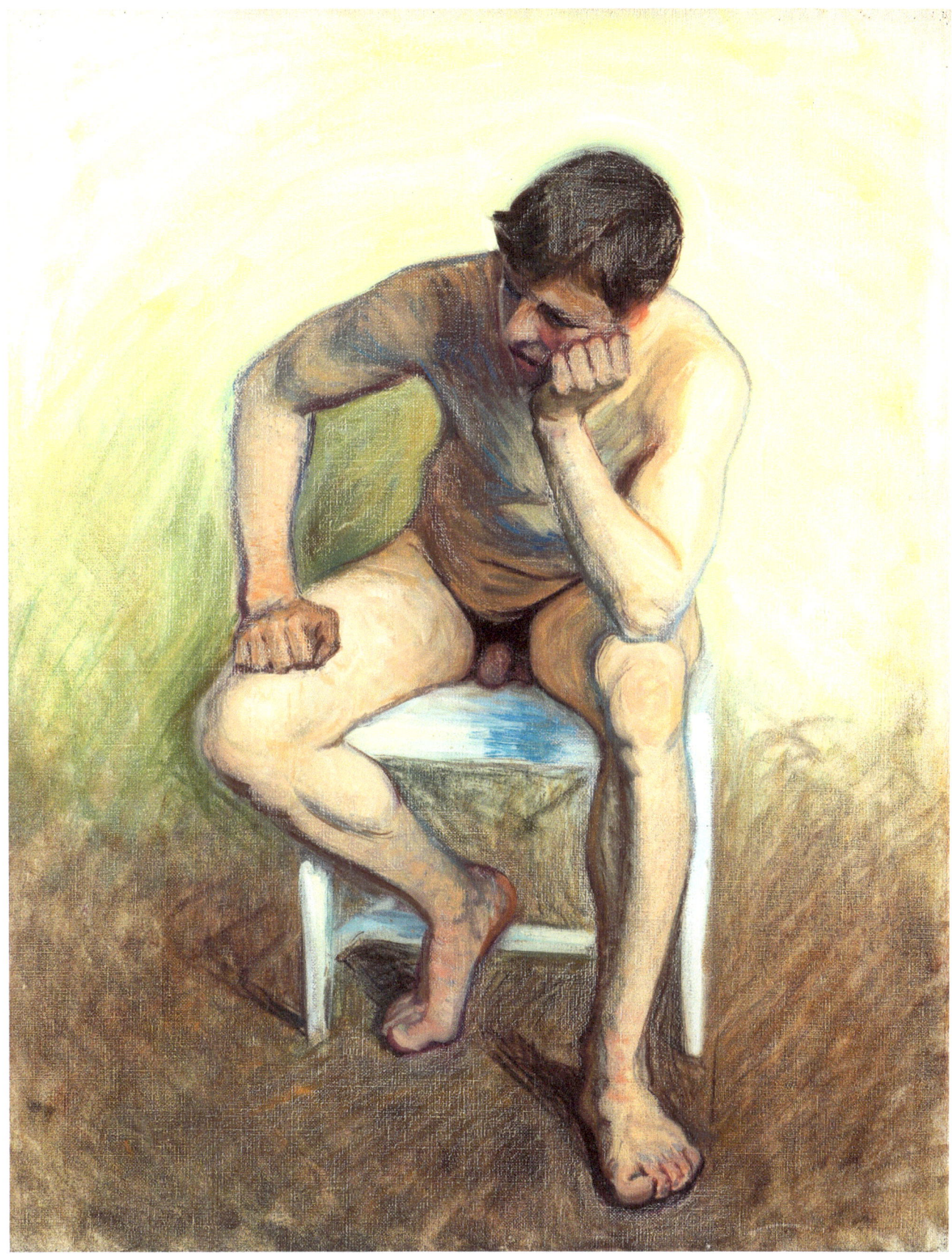

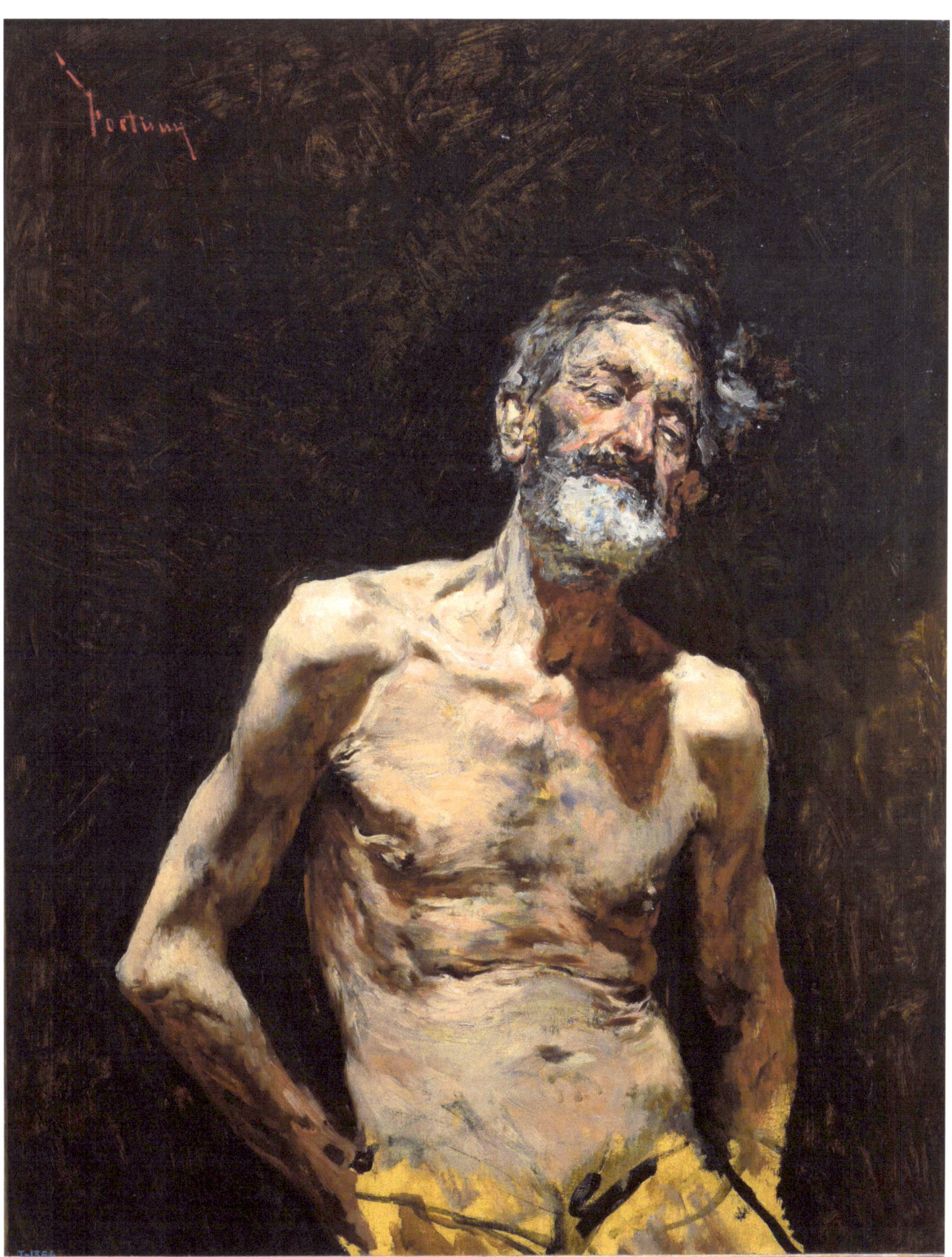

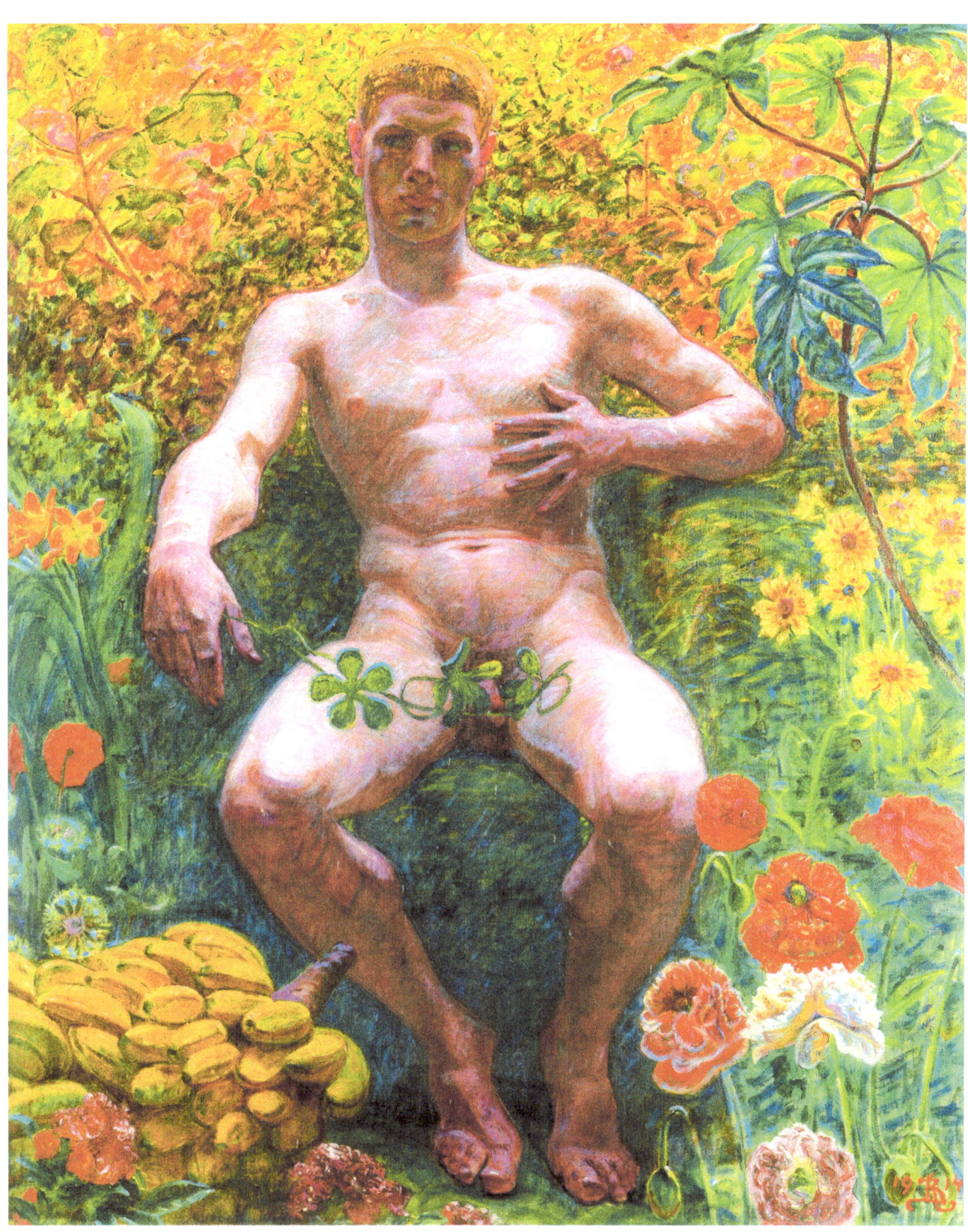

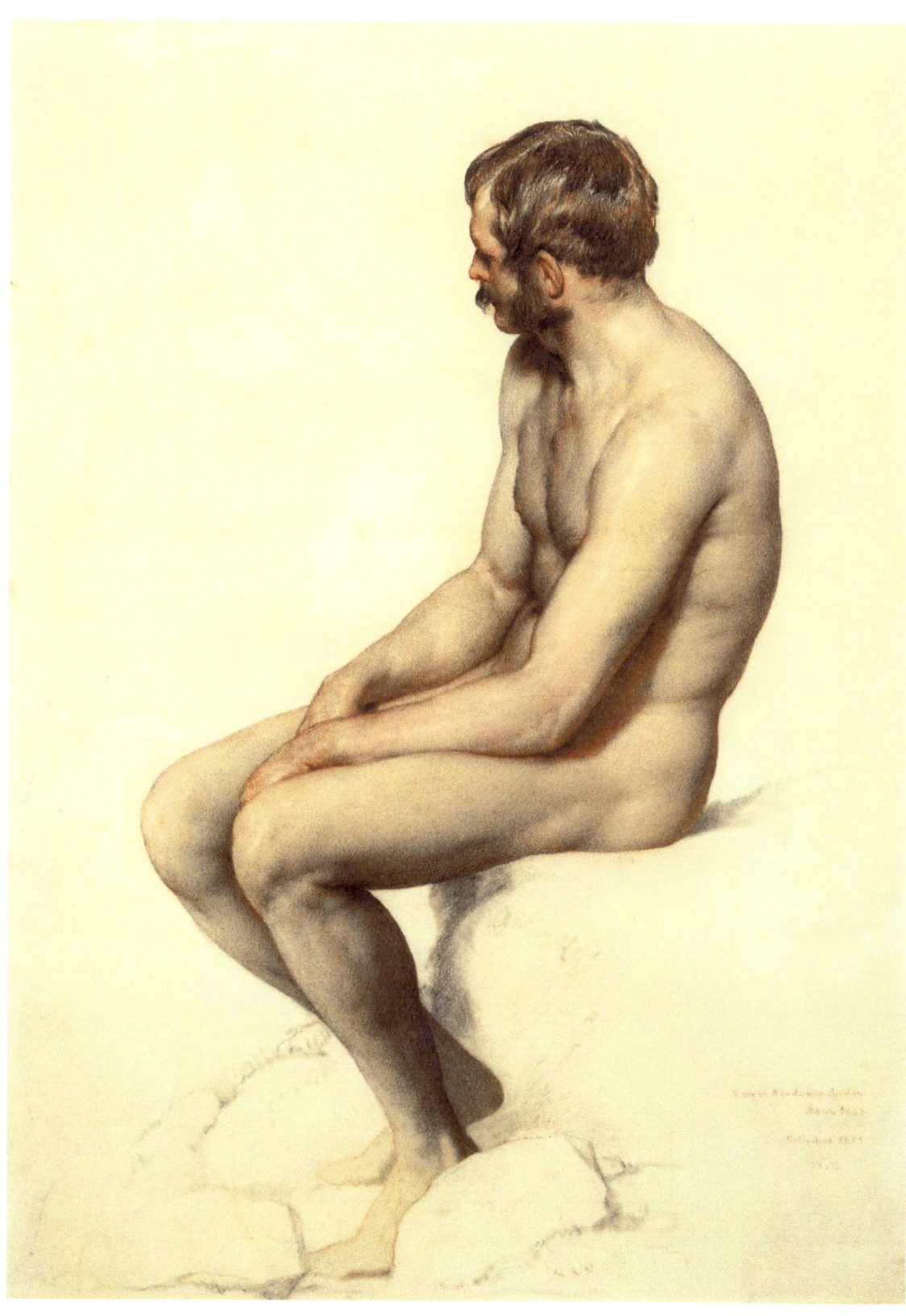

OPPOSITE PAGE:
TITLE: Standing Male Model, Carl Frørup
ARTIST: Christoffer Wilhelm Eckersberg
YEAR: 1837

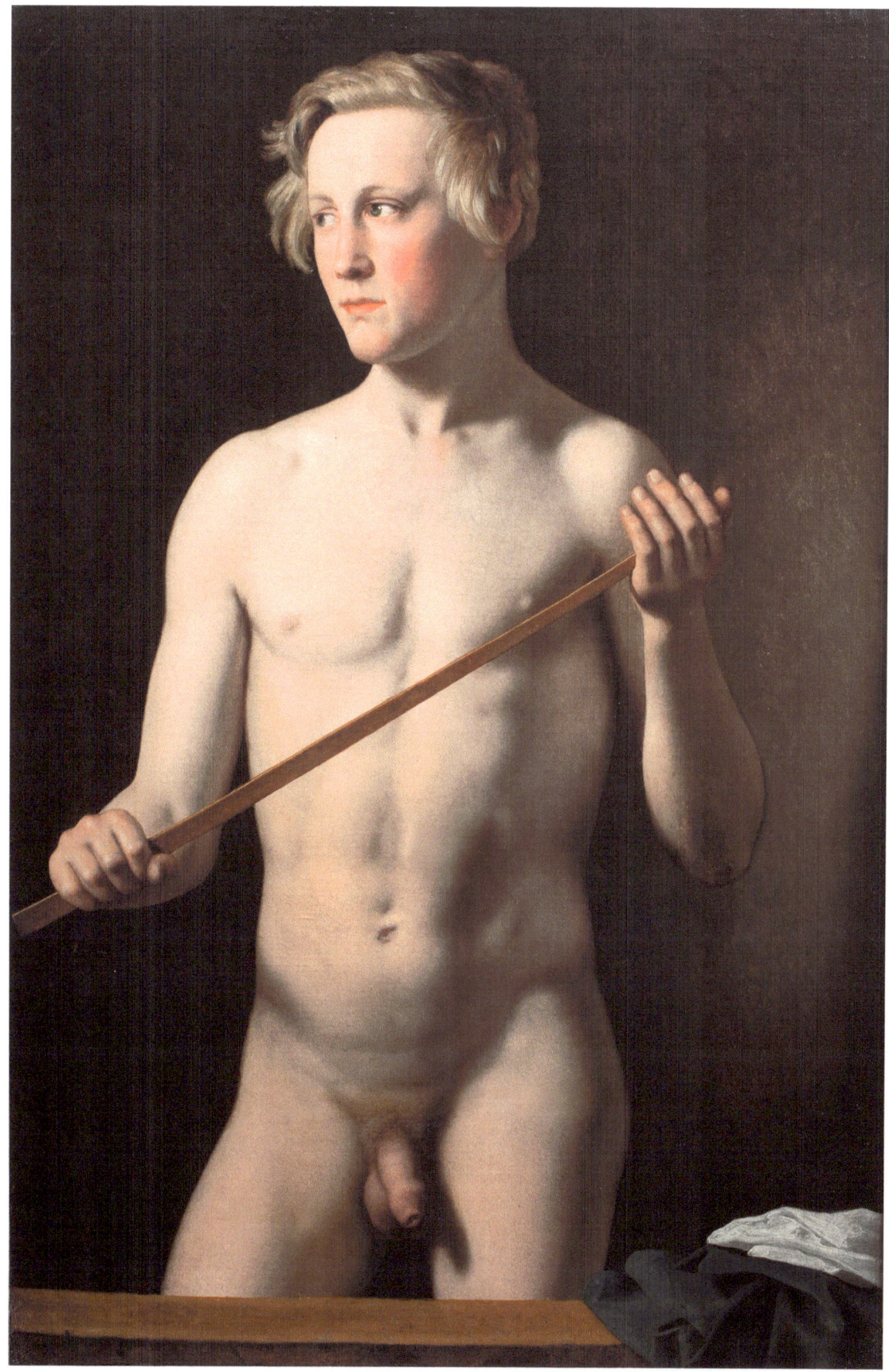

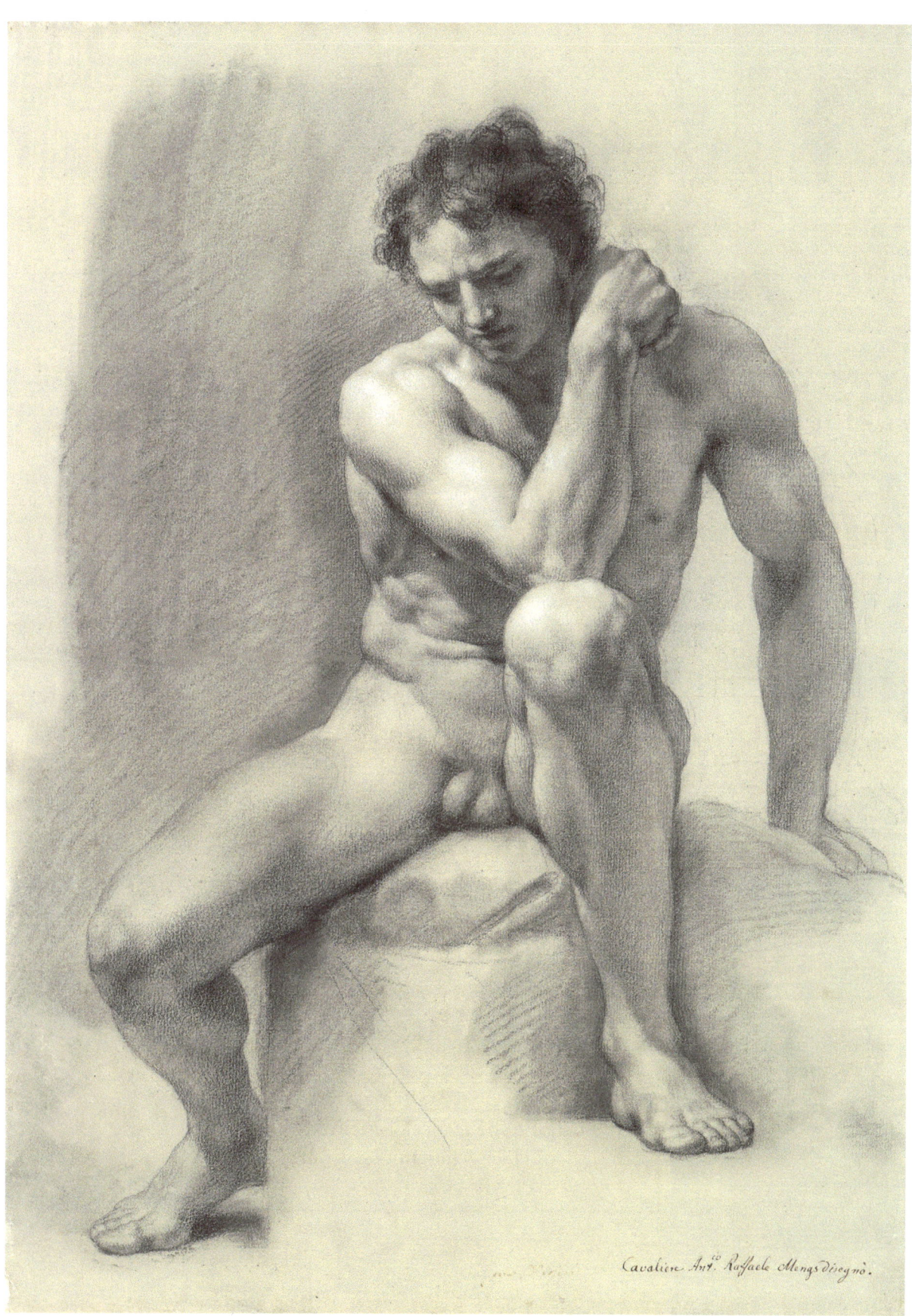

Cavaliere Anto. Raffaele Mengs disegnò.

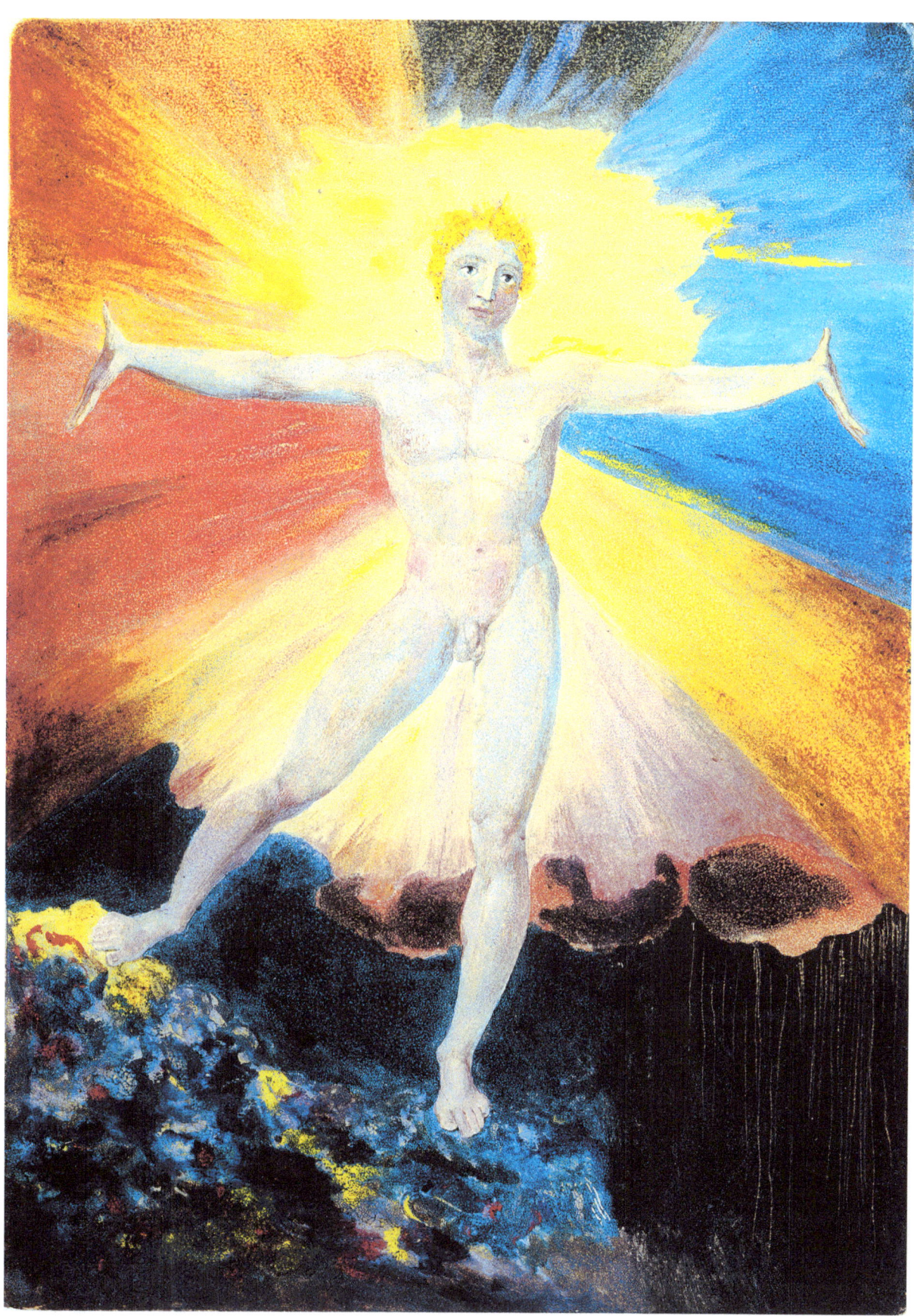

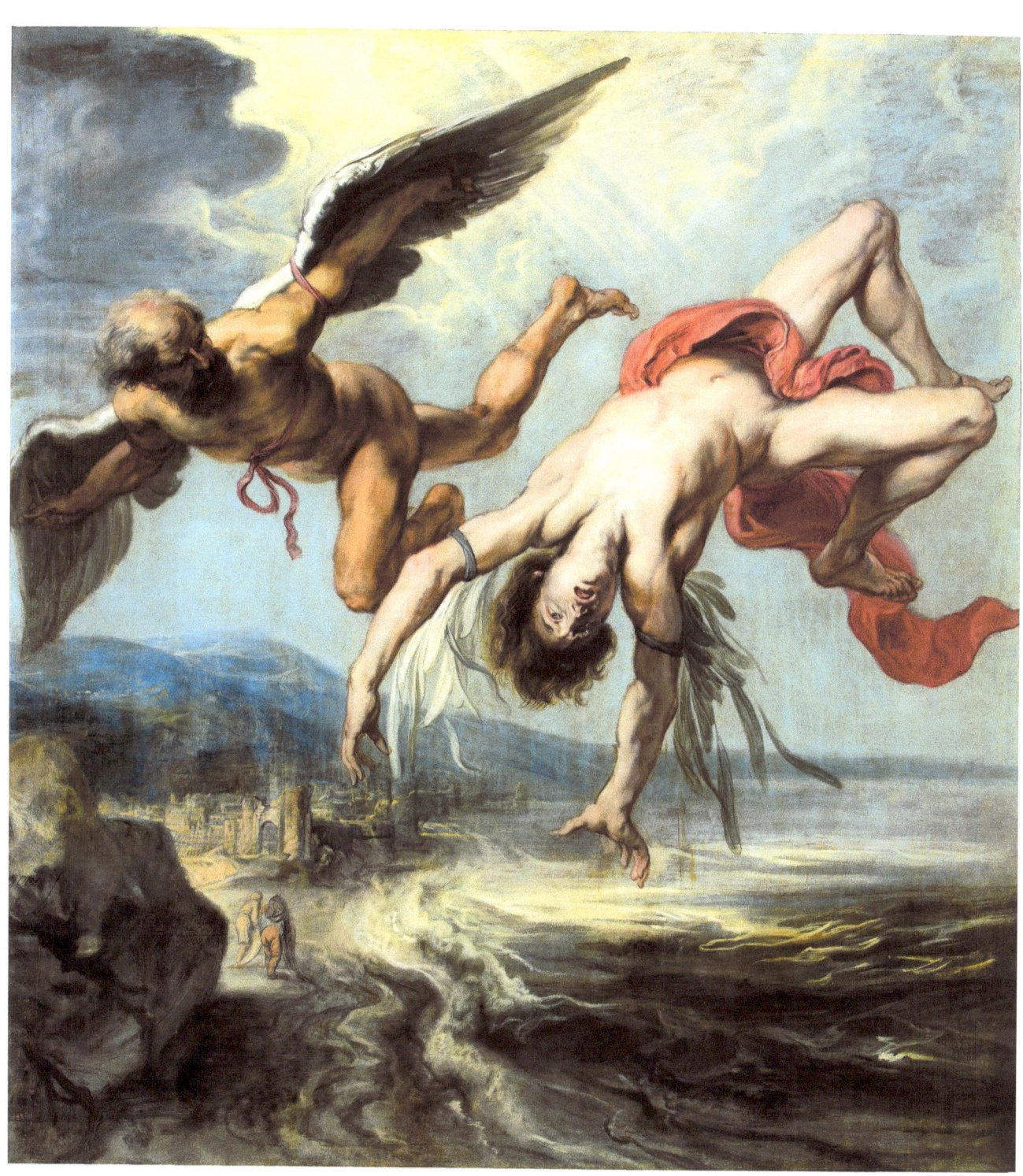

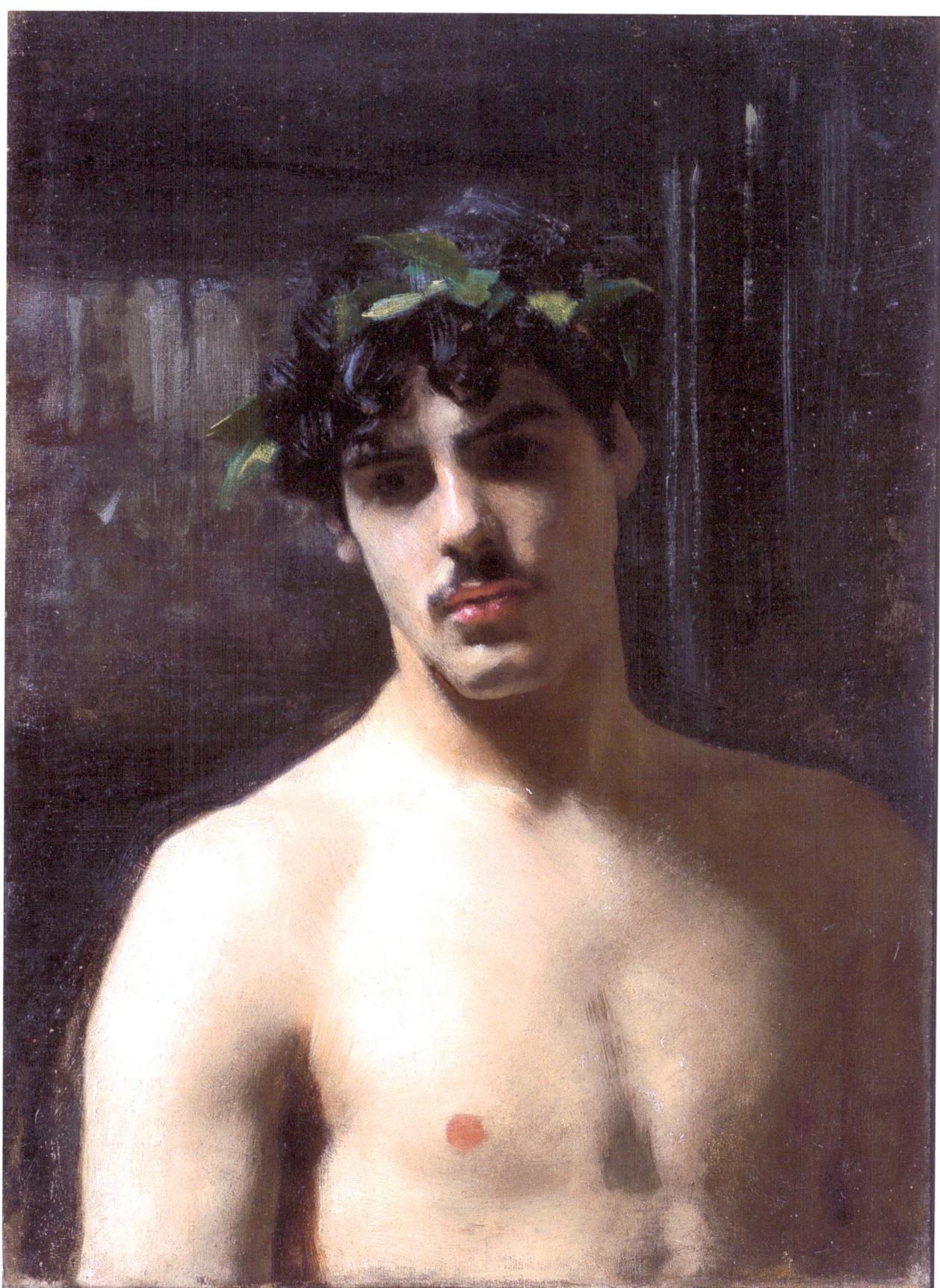

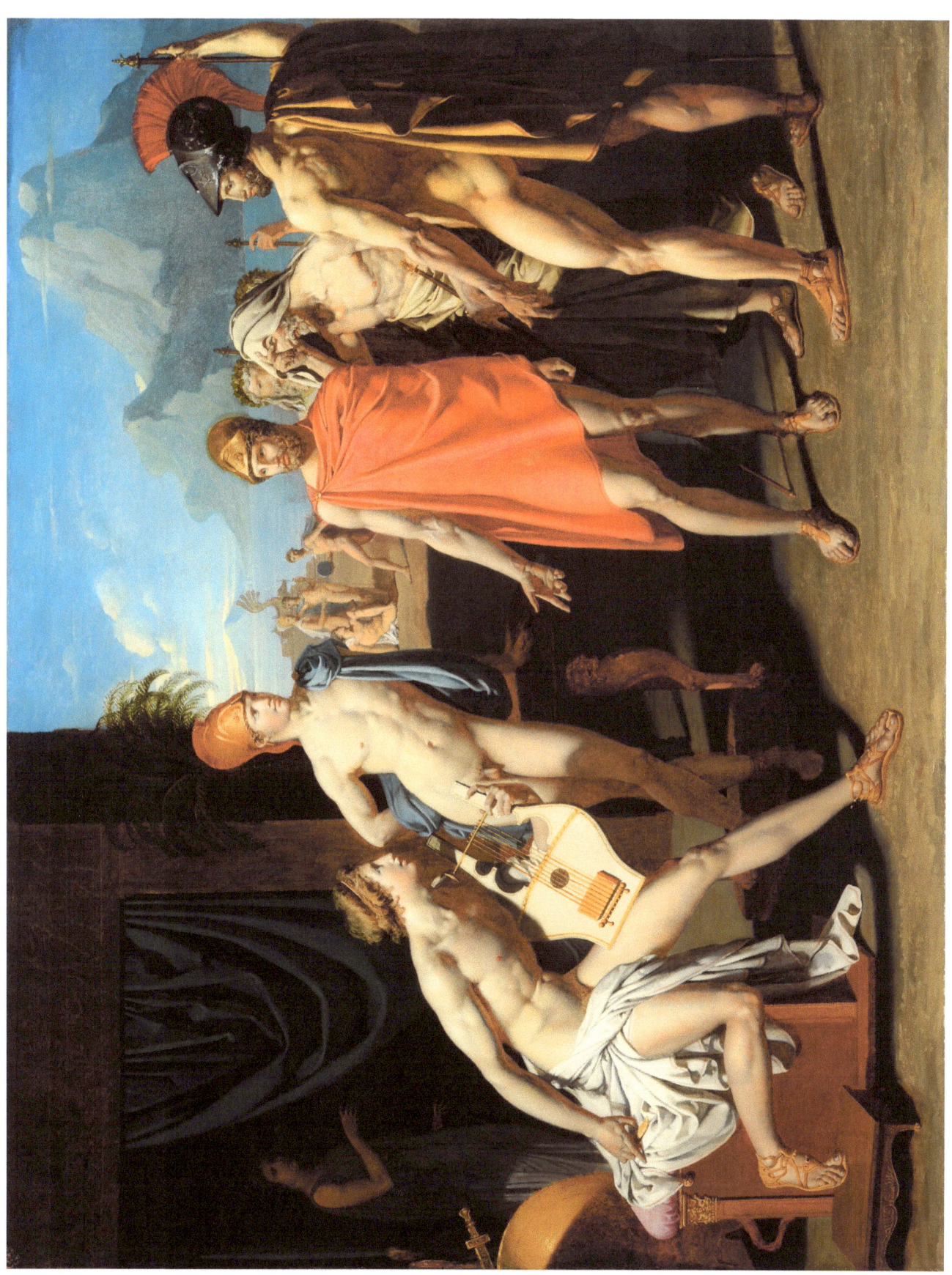

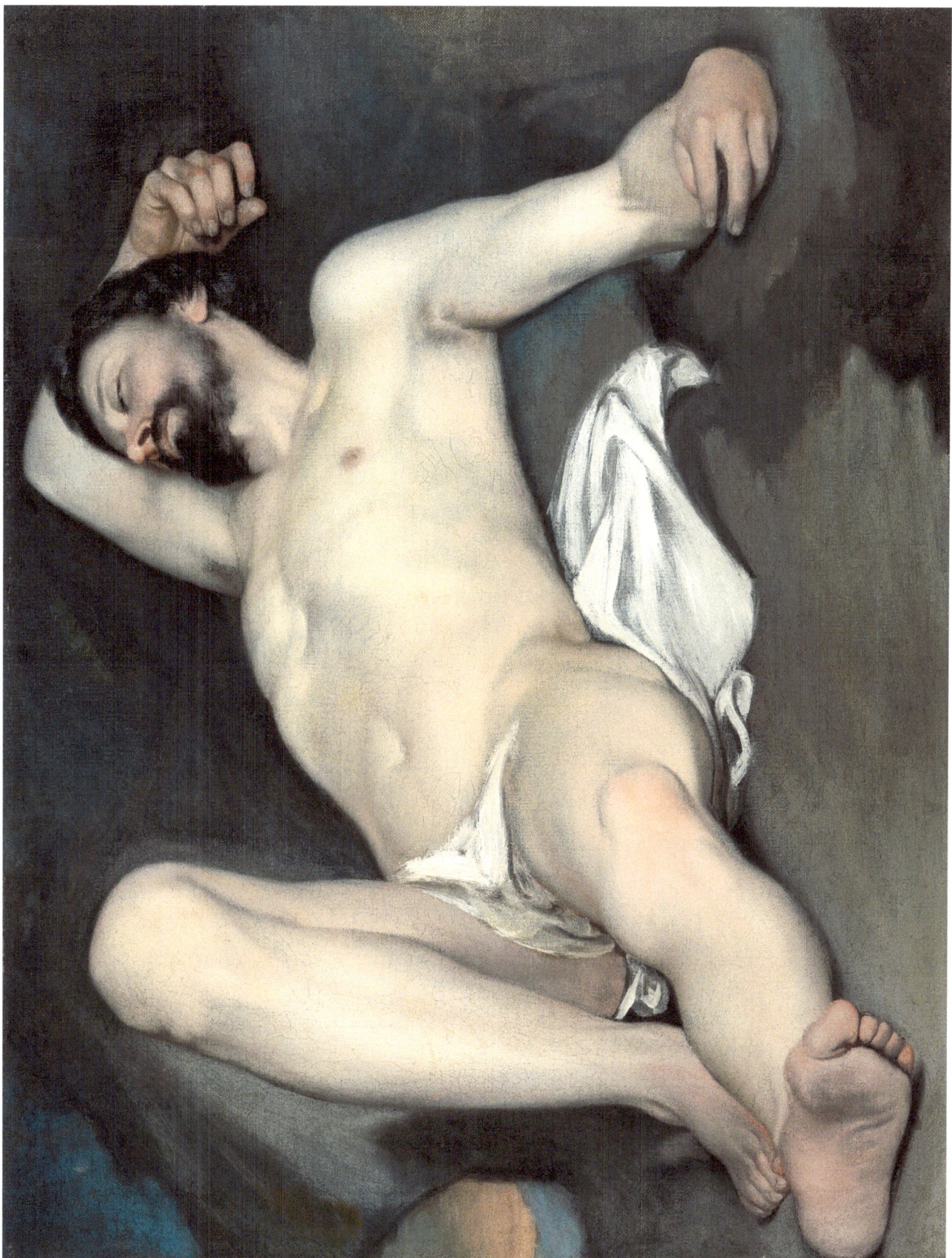

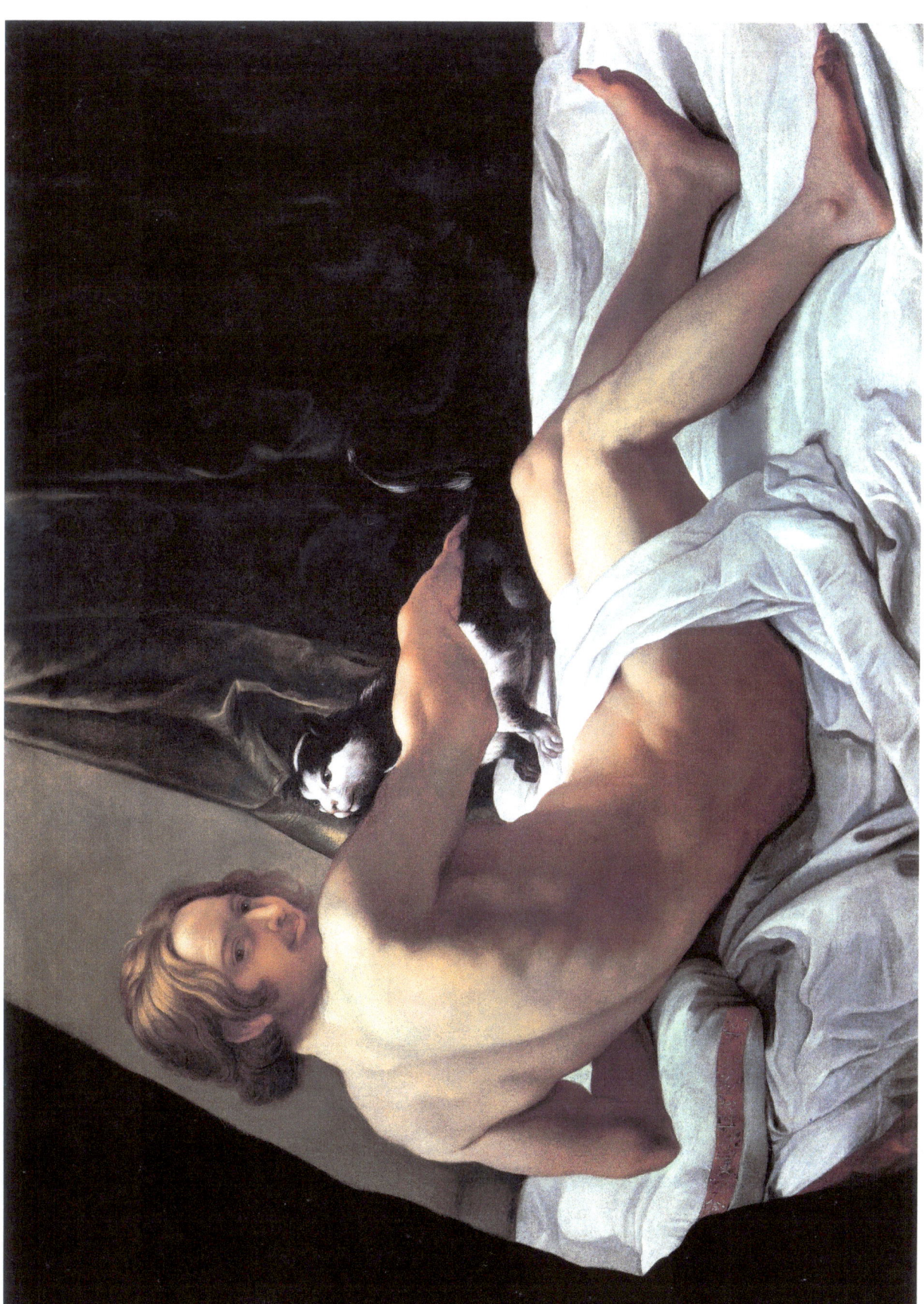

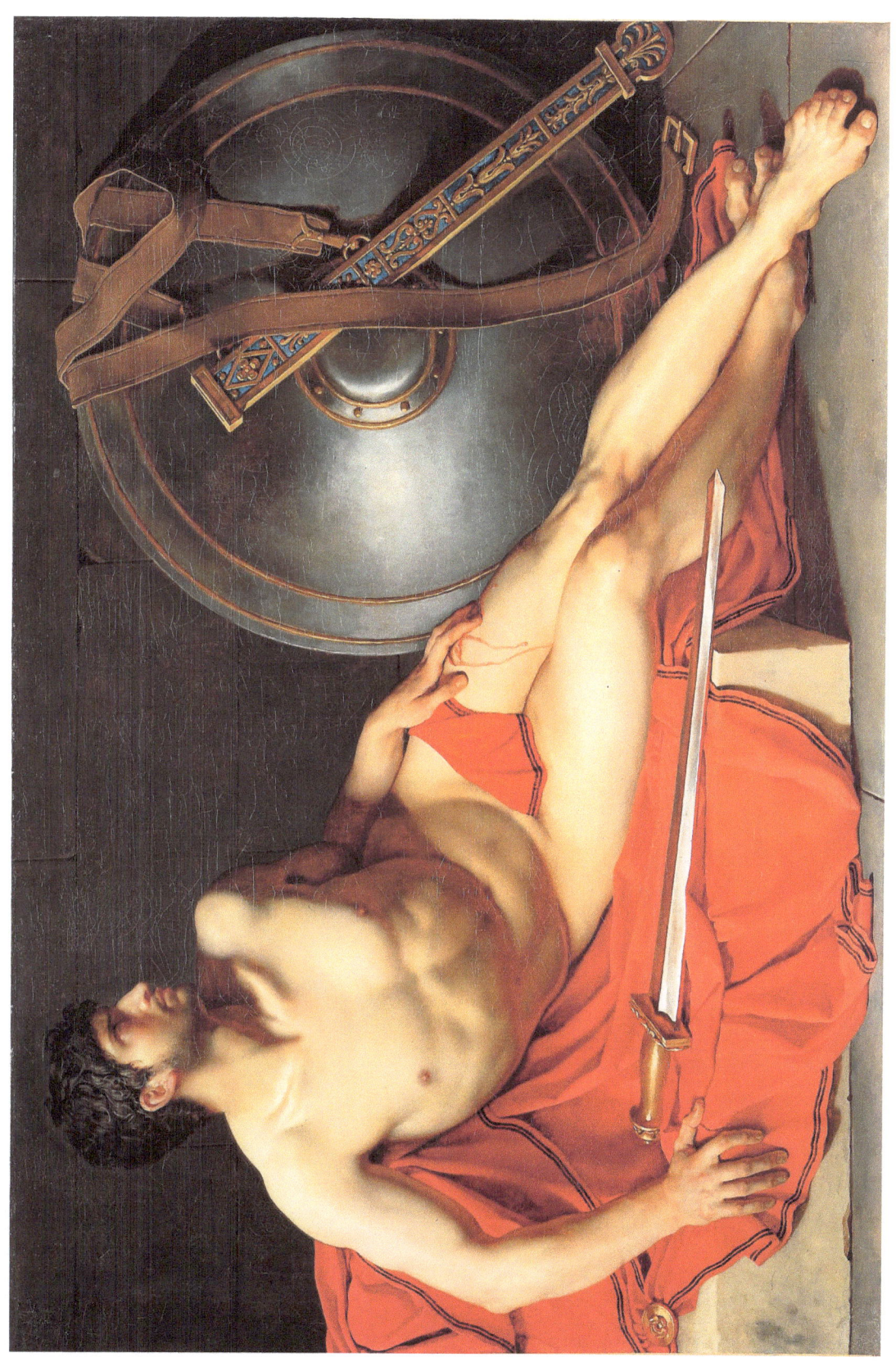

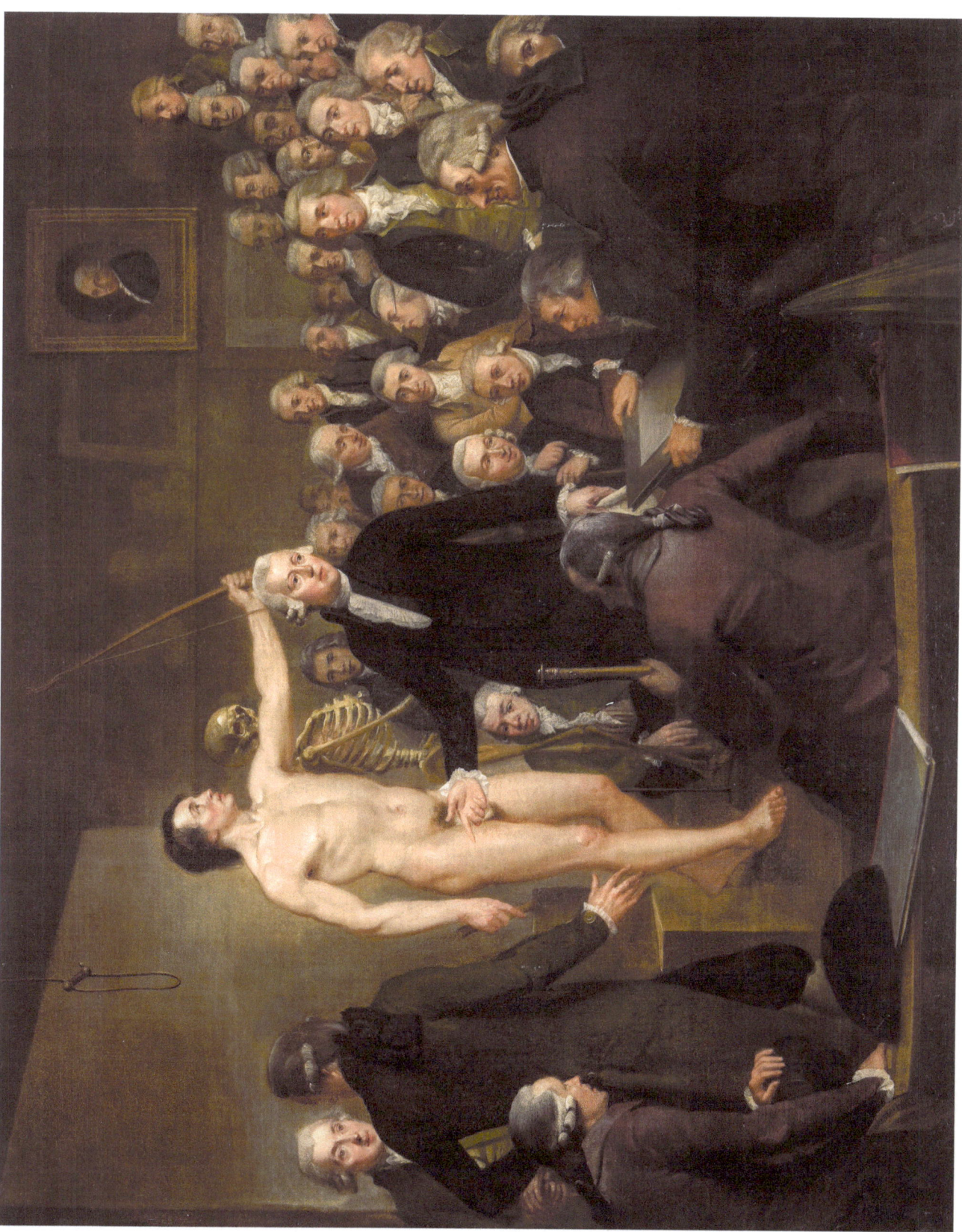

OPPOSITE PAGE:
TITLE: Wrestlers
ARTIST: Thomas Eakins
YEAR: 1899

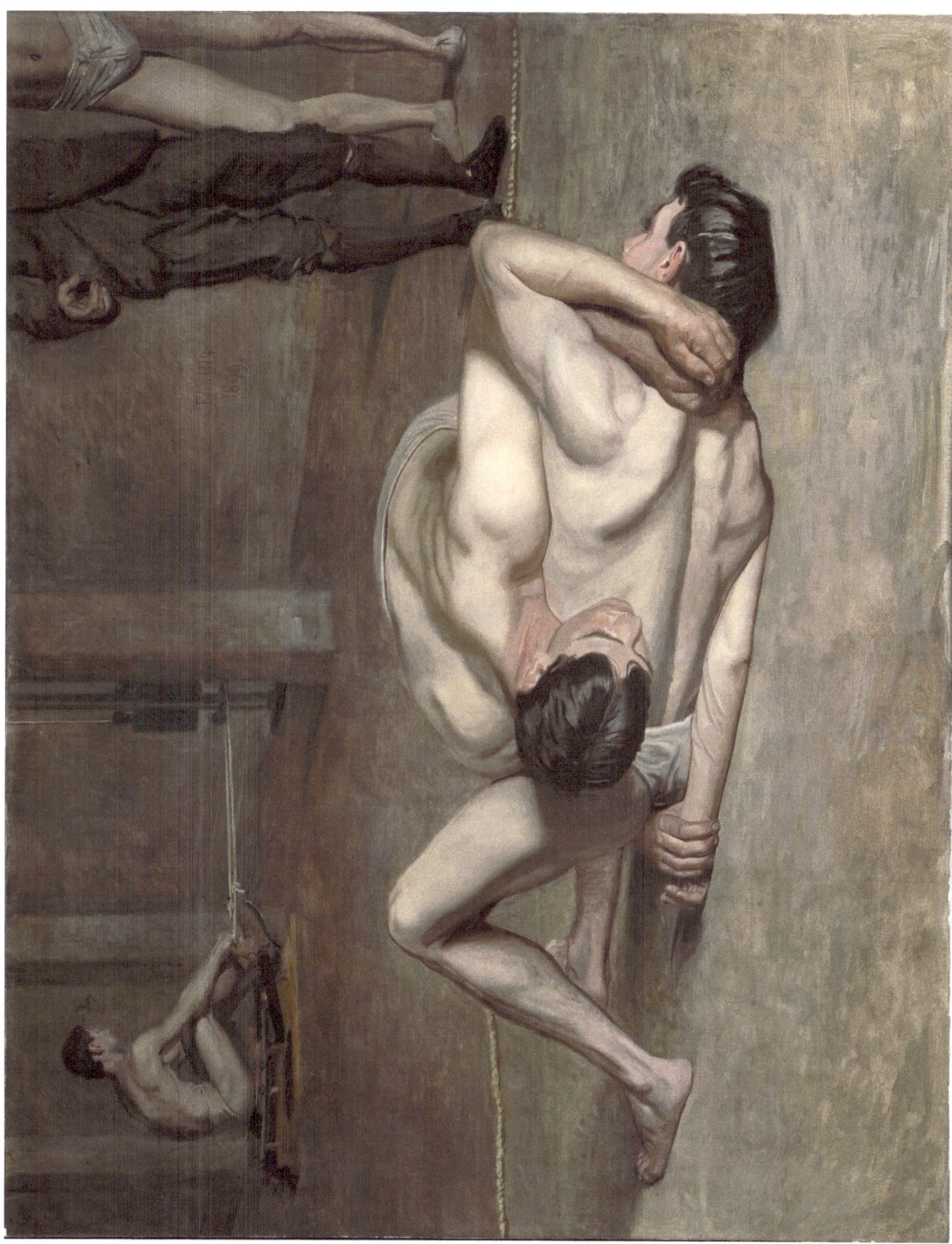

OPPOSITE PAGE:
TITLE: Drunkenness of Noah
ARTIST: The Bolognese School
YEAR: 17th Century

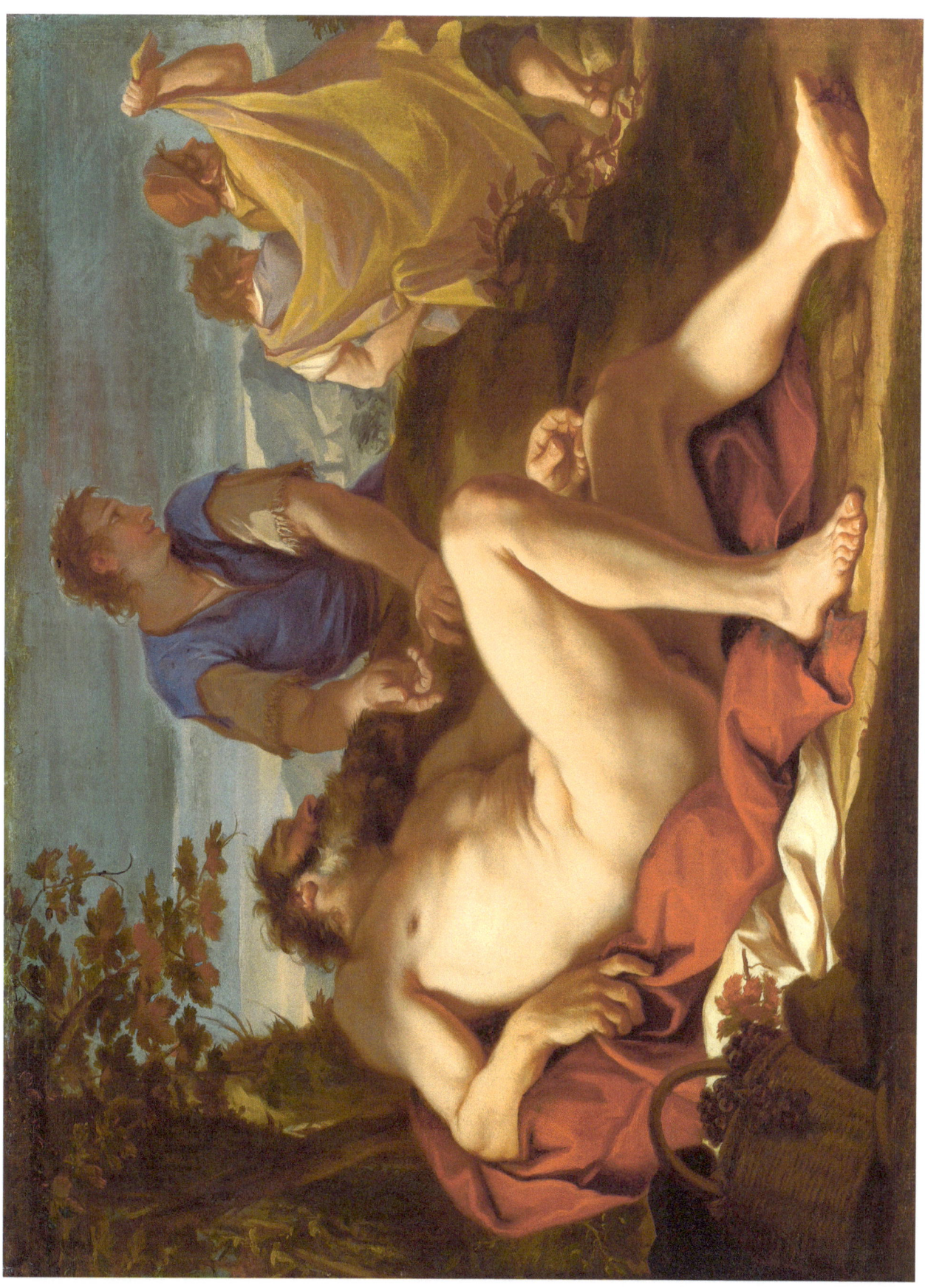

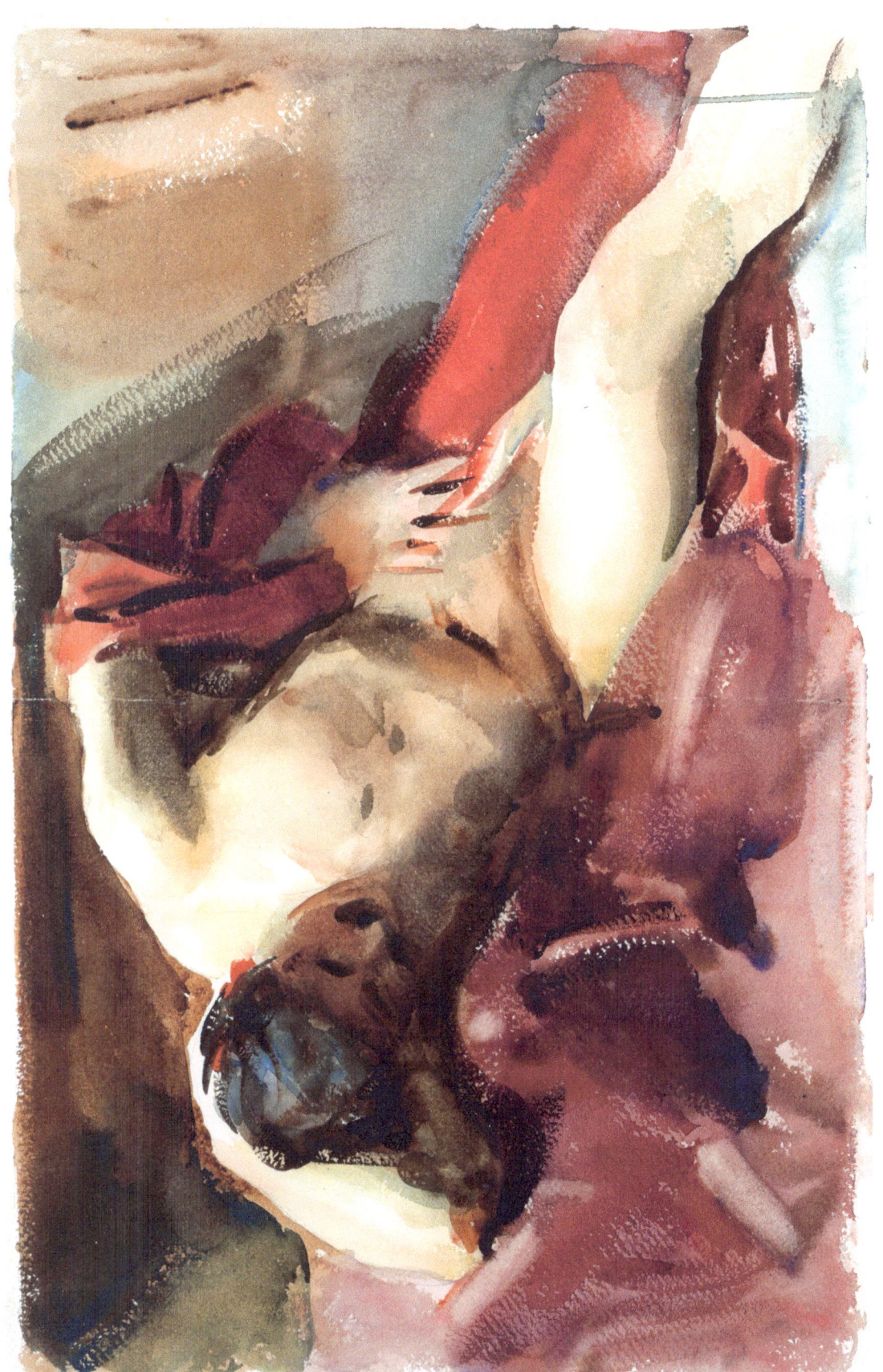

OPPOSITE PAGE:
TITLE: Sleeping Endymion
ARTIST: Nicolas-Guy Brenet
YEAR: 1756

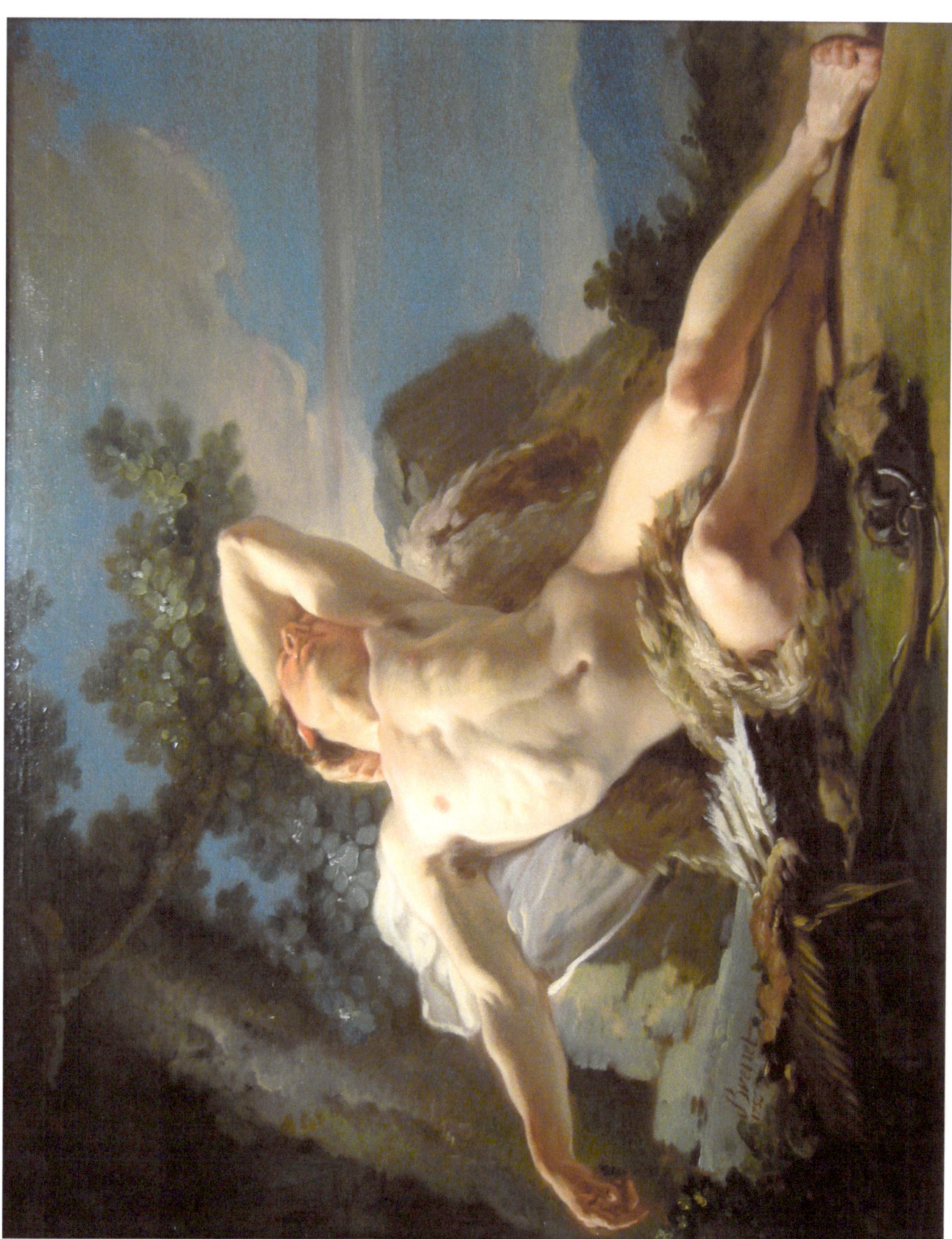

OPPOSITE PAGE:
TITLE: The Fall of the Titans
ARTIST: Cornelis van Haarlem
YEAR: between 1588-1590

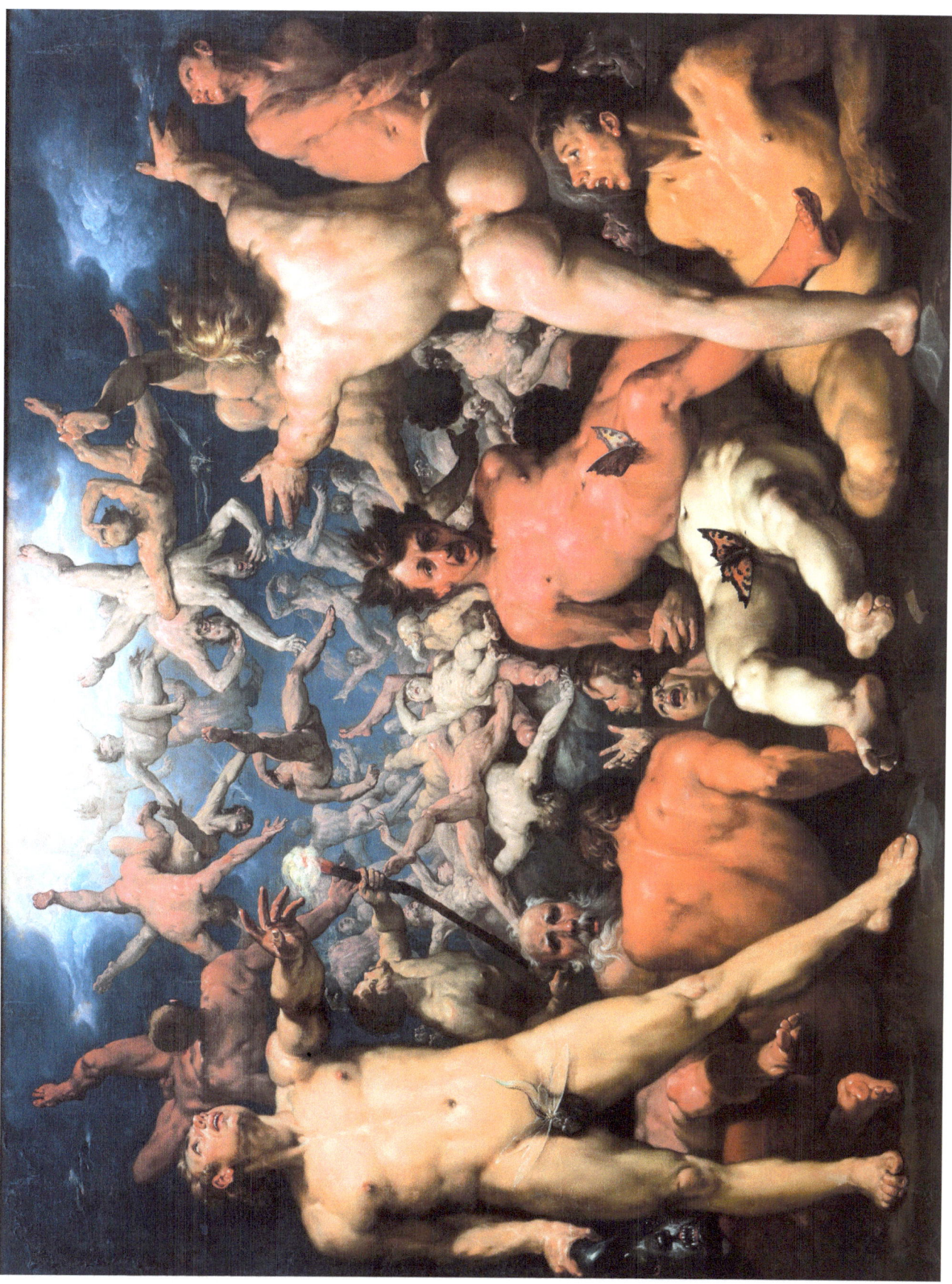

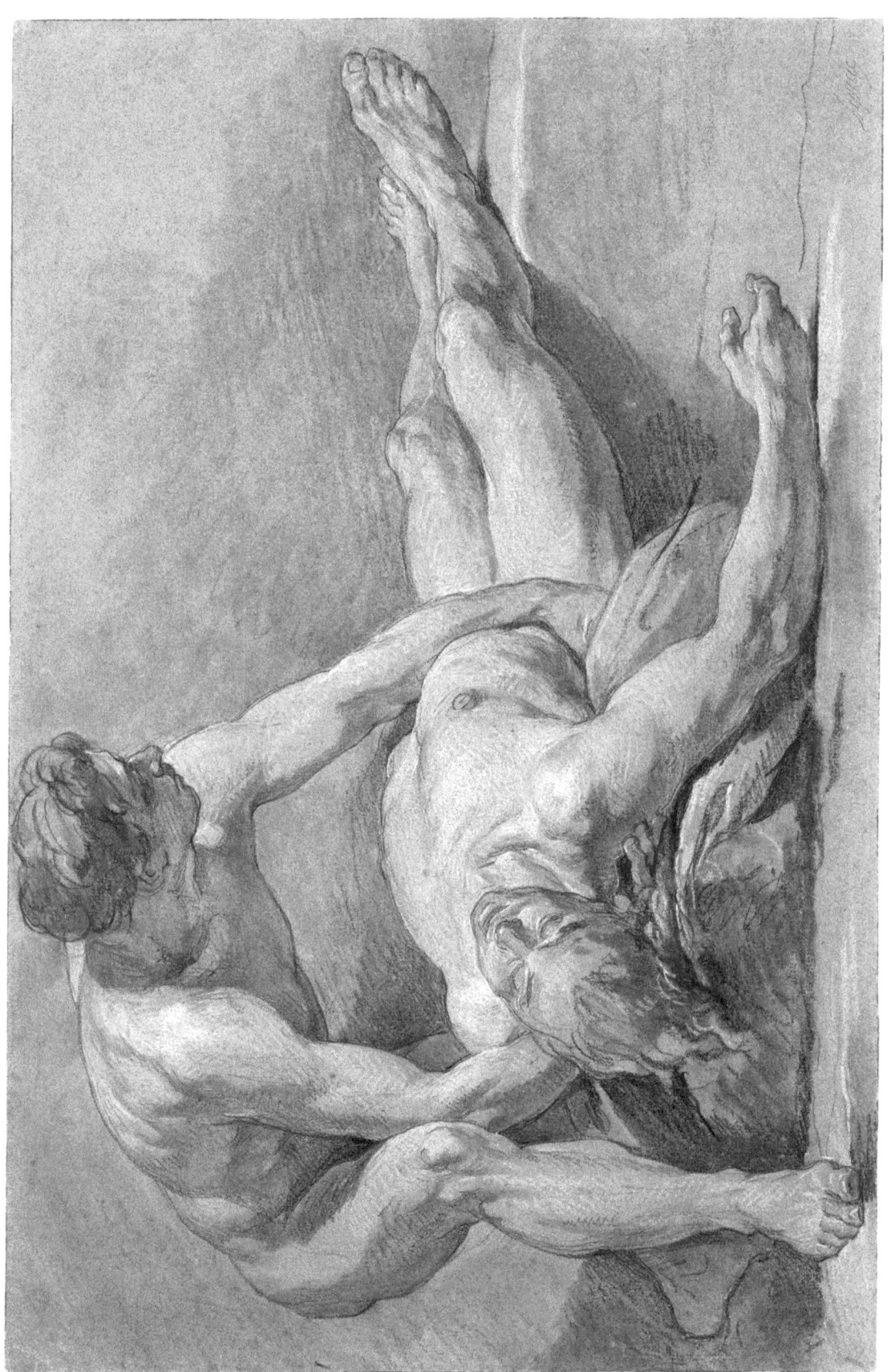

OPPOSITE PAGE:
TITLE: La colère d' Achille (The Wrath of Achilles)
ARTIST: Michel Martin Drolling
YEAR: 1810

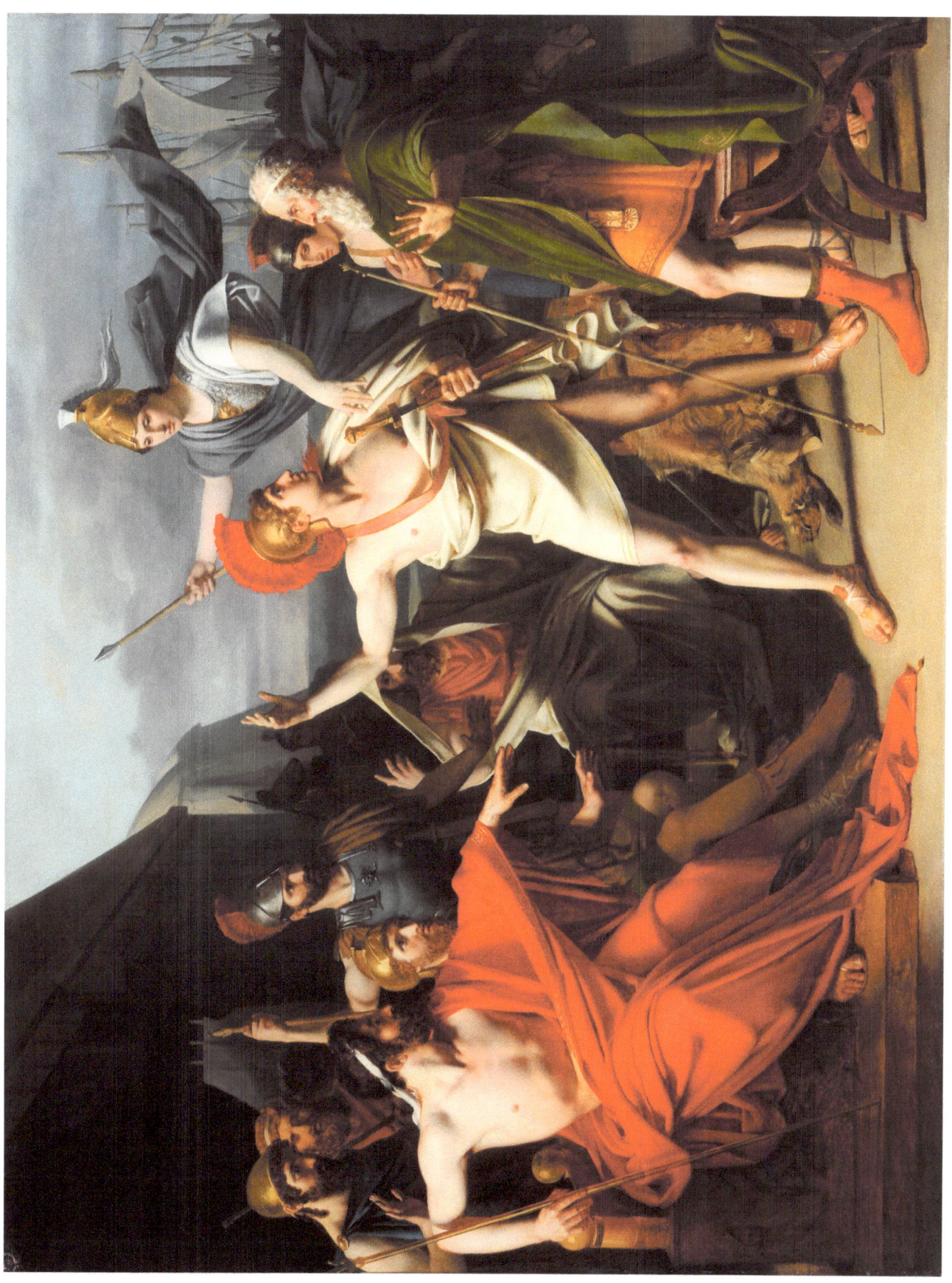

OPPOSITE PAGE:
TITLE: Swimming
ARTIST: Thomas Eakins
YEAR: between 1884-1885

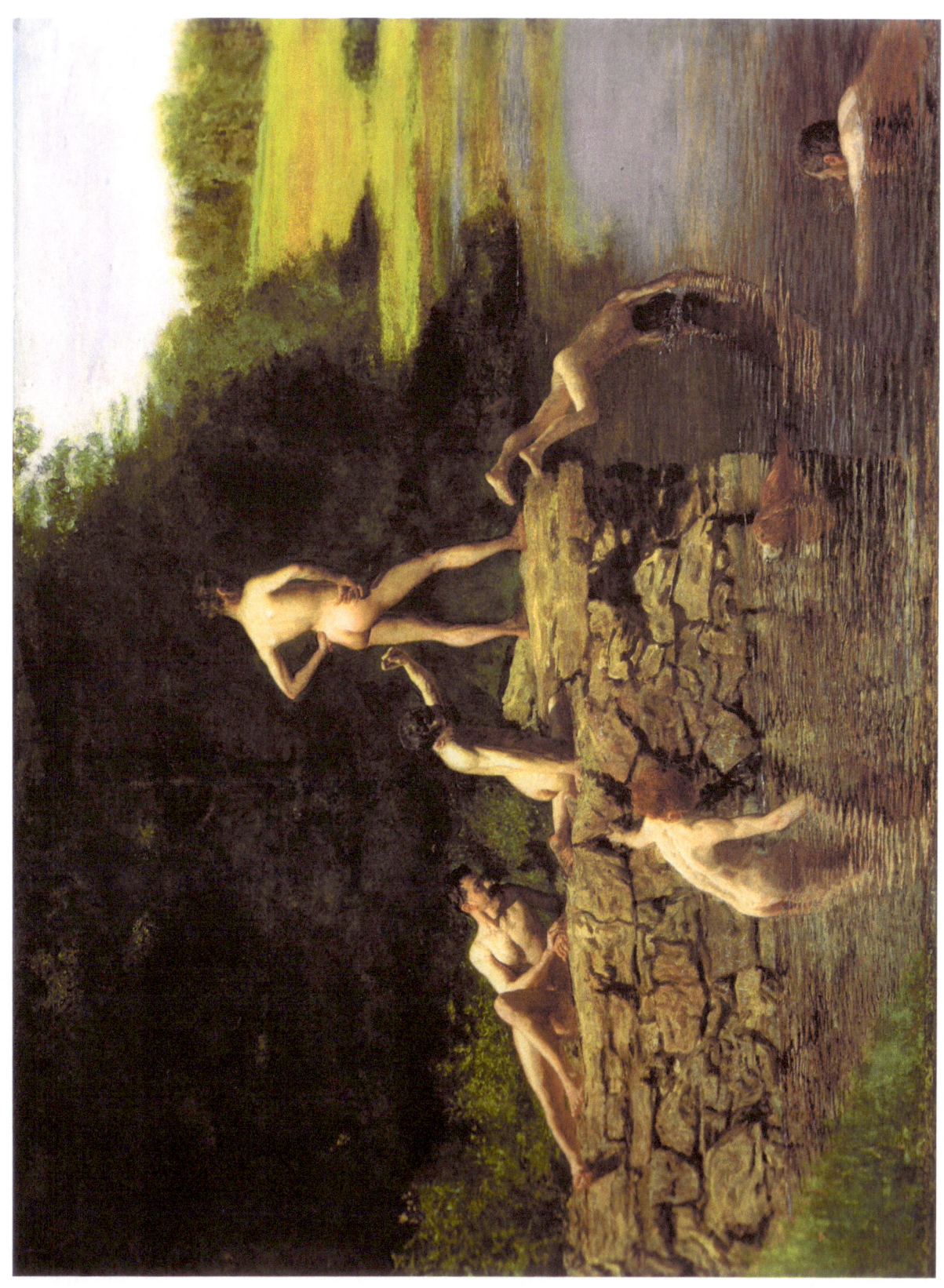

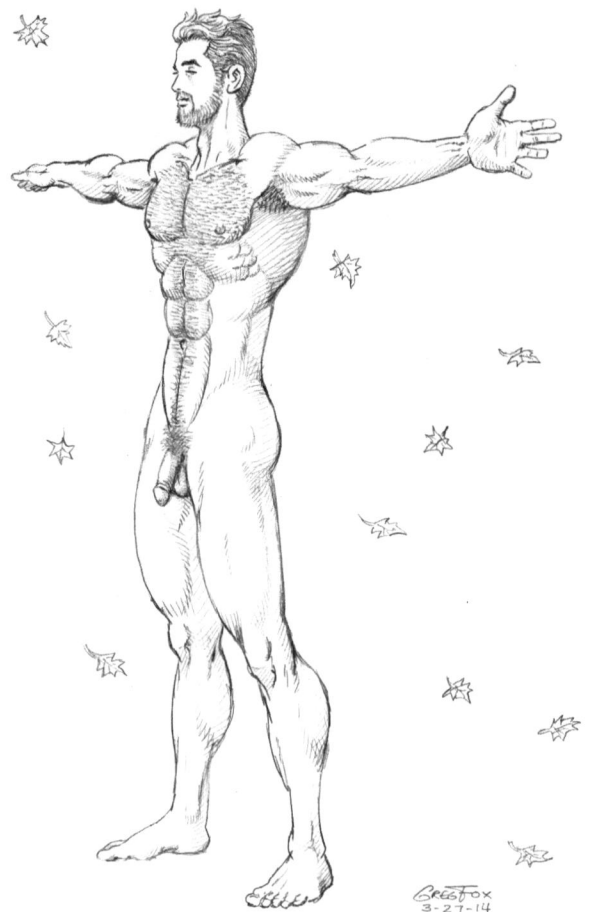

"Drew Danvers in the
Autumn Breeze"
pencil drawing
by Greg Fox
2014

PAGE REMOVAL SUGGESTIONS:

So, you want to frame some of these beautiful art prints and get 'em up on your walls to beautify your home or workplace? Cool! Here are 2 methods to get individual pages out of this book smoothly & easily. I prefer method # 1, but if that seems too tricky, (or if you're at all nervous about or unskilled with using a razor blade), try method # 2.

Method # 1

What you'll need:

- A sharp cutting tool, such as an X-acto knife, box cutter, or even a fresh razor blade.
- A thin, solid surface to place behind the page you're going to remove from the book. It must be longer than the height of the book, (11 inches). A thin metal ruler would be ideal. If you don't have that, a thin manila folder or very thin piece of cardboard will do, as long as it's slightly longer than 11 inches).
- If you're at all nervous about cutting yourself with that razor, a pair of semi-heavy work gloves, (check out Home Depot for a large variety).

Now follow these directions:

1. Place the book on a firm table surface in front of you, and open it to the page of the art print you want to remove from the book.
2. Now, turn the page one page ahead, and place your thin solid surface, (the metal ruler or manila folder), on that page.
3. Push the metal ruler/manila folder as far into the inner center binding of the book as you can, and hold it there in place.
4. Turn back to the page of the art print you want to remove, so that the art print is now facing you, and the metal ruler/manila folder is directly behind it, pressed into the inner center binding of the book.
5. Now, with the book held open as WIDE as you can manage, **VERY CAREFULLY**, take your sharp cutting tool, and, (placing it as close as you can to the inner center binding of the book), beginning at the bottom of the page, slice upward to the top of the page. Be sure to make the slice as CLOSE to the inner center binding of the book as you can
6. Once you've removed the page from the book…take a deep breath. You did it!

Method # 2

What you'll need:

- String, (just some plain white string, like kite string or any string, really, as long as it's clean).
- A glass of clean water.

Now follow these directions:
1. Cut a length of string longer than the book's height, (11 inches.... cut it to about 14 inches, so there's extra to hold on to).
2. Soak the string in the glass of clean water. It needs to be wet, although it shouldn't be dripping wet, as that may be too much. Just get it nice and wet, but not dripping.
3. Open the book to the page of the art print you want to remove. Place the wet string **along the very inner center binding** of the book on that page; pull it tight so it is straight, very firmly tucked into the inner binding, **as close to the inner spine as possible**, (this is **important**!).
4. Close the book and hold it tightly closed for about 15 seconds.
5. Now open the book, remove the string and examine the page. There should be a line where the string was where it is wet, and therefore very weak.
6. Now carefully tear the page out . It should tear cleanly on the line. if not, wet the string more and put it back on the already weak area and do it again. (The edge of the page you tore may look a little ragged, but that's OK... that part will be hidden under the matte part of the frame).

Why do I NOT prefer this method? Well, I'm a bit nervous about getting any kind of water near my books, and while this amount of water is miniscule and should not damage the rest of the book, it still makes me a little nervous about long term effects on the book itself. However, if you're planning to frame ALL or most of the art prints in the book, and saving the book itself is not important, then by all means, I would use this method. (You can always buy another copy of this book if you want to have it in book form, while also having the prints hanging on your wall!).

A quick note about FRAMING and HANGING these art-prints ......
The frame size you'll need to frame these is the standard 8" x 10" picture-frame; the kind that have a matte inside, which actually allows for a slightly smaller viewing area of 7 and 3/8" x 9 and 3/8". This is a very standard frame size, probably the most common size you'll find in stores, (and conveniently, the right size for ALL of the art-prints in this book!). My advice… if you happen to have a **Michael's** arts & crafts store in your area, they have a wonderful selection of frames, at very affordable prices, (which often go on sale… it may pay to check their sale flyer for several weeks before buying. I've often bought frames there at 50% off!).

After you've (very carefully) removed the art print you want to frame from this book, just center it within the cardboard matte that comes with your frame, (hint: use a couple of pieces of low-resistant artist's or painter's tape to hold it in place), place it within your frame, and you're all set!

When choosing a wall on which to hang your art print, (and this goes for **all** other prints, photos, and original artwork, too, that you may want to hang in your home or workspace), always choose a surface that does **not** get hit by **direct sunlight,** as that could eventually fade the print/photo/ artwork. You may need to take a few days to check a wall surface at various times of the day, as some areas may only get exposed to direct sunlight for a few hours a day, such as early morning or late afternoon, which can still be damaging. (This is especially important for o**riginal artwork**... because if an art print or photo gets sun-damaged, you could always buy another book of prints or photos to replace it... but once original artwork is damaged, it's irreplaceable). Now you know all you need to know to beautify your home or workspace with inspiring artwork!!!

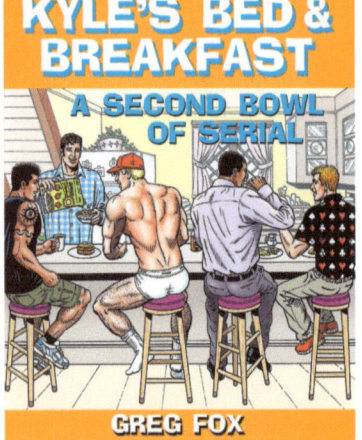
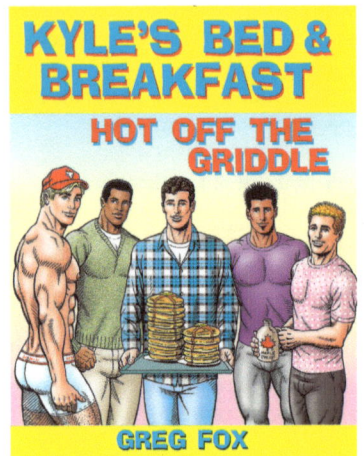
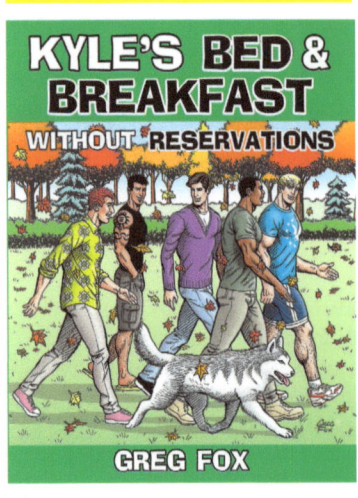

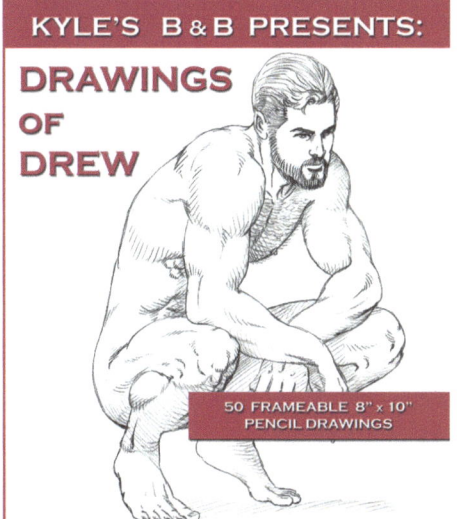
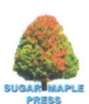
ACKNOWLEDGEMENTS

There are so many to thank for helping this book come to be. Starting with

- My mother, Eleanor, whose life was filled with appreciation of art and made our home an art-filled, beautiful, warm place to live. I miss you every day!

- Aunt Sheila, who was such an empowering, artful influence on me all throughout my life… I miss you every day, too!

- The rest of my family, in New York, California, and beyond. Thank you for your love and belief in me.

- Book Revue bookstore in Huntington, Long Island, NY. My "second home" for so many years!
- My friends far and wide… from Huntington, Geneseo, Spize, Sam Ash, Northport, Book Revue, the Berndt Toast gang, Prism Comics, the Comic Con circuit and elsewhere. Thank you for lifting me up and making me smile!
- For the many artists whose amazing work is featured in this book. Thank you for sharing your tremendous talent, which brought light into this world… I am deeply honored to be able to present your work once again for the world to appreciate!
- Kathy O'Marra, for being such a strong supporter of my work all these years. And for being a great friend!
- My friend Grant Thatcher, for not flinching when I continually asked for his opinion on yet another cover design!!!
- Misty, Ginger, and Midnight
- Marianne Williamson, for your inspiration and for being a sparkling light in this world.
- The readers of Kyle's B&B. Thank you for your love and support of my art… I am deeply, deeply grateful.
- Jesus, the Holy Spirit, and all of the Angels and saints!
- God, for all of the love, light, and joy. And for so many miracles along the way!

♥ KEEP YOUR LOVE ALIVE ♥

If you happen to be looking for any organizations that are doing good work in the world, here are just a few, (of many), that I heartily encourage you to visit their websites and find out more about:

- www.doctorswithoutborders.org   **Doctors Without Borders,** (Médecins Sans Frontières), Providing emergency medical care around the world in desperate situations.

- www.oxfamamerica.org   **Oxfam** is an international confederation of 15 organizations working in more than 90 countries worldwide to find lasting solutions to poverty and related injustice around Providing emergency medical care around the world in desperate situations.

- www.glwd.org   **God's Love We Deliver** is the tri-state area's, (NY, NJ, CT). leading provider of nutritious, individually-tailored meals to people who are too sick to shop or cook for themselves.

- www.outrightinternational.org   **OutRight Action International** (formerly the International Gay & Lesbian Human Rights Campaign)

- www.TheHungerSite.com   (Click & Donate Free Food!)

- www.gmhc.org   **The Gay Men's Health Crisis** (GMHC) is a NYC-based non-profit, volunteer-supported and community-based AIDS service organization that has led the United States in the fight against AIDS.

- www.whyhunger.org   **Why Hunger** (formerly World Hunger Year). Working to eradicate world hunger.

- www.nrdc.org   **(National Resource Defense Council)** NRDC's mission is to safeguard the Earth: its people, its plants and animals and the natural systems on which all life depends.

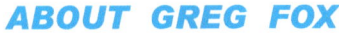

ABOUT GREG FOX

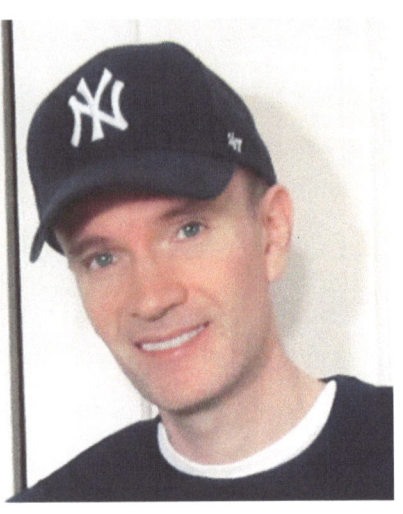

Greg Fox began making comics at 12 years old, publishing his first strip at age 14 in his high school newspaper and continuing to illustrate and write comic strips through high school and college. He received a B.A. from Geneseo College in upstate New York. Immediately following college, he played guitar in several New York-based rock bands, but then jumped into doing comics full-force. His illustration work has appeared in comic books for a number of companies, including Triumphant Comics, and Marvel Comics, and in magazines such as Blue, the Advocate, Genre, D.J. Times, Music & Sound Retailer, and many others. He is also the writer/artist for such comic strips as "**Manic Music**", (based on his experience in the rock music world), and "**An Angel's Story**".

Fox's most notable comic strip, "**Kyle's Bed & Breakfast**", premiered in late 1998. The strip is currently syndicated to a variety of publications across North America, and also has a worldwide following on the web. Since 2004, Fox has published 4 book collections of Kyle's B&B, (one of which was a Lambda Literary Award Finalist), and an addictional volume of classical-style figure drawings of Drew Danvers, one of the characters in Kyle's B&B, He was the grand-prize winner of the "Life Without Fair Courts" cartoon contest in 2007, sponsored by Lambda Legal. **The Sugar Maple Press Anthology of Nature Poems**, published in Spring of 2014, featured Greg Fox as editor and photographer. The fourth collection of Kyle's B&B , "Kyle's Bed & Breakfast: Without Reservations" was published in November, 2015.

Fox currently resides in Northport, Long Island, New York, busily working on new episodes of Kyle's B&B, and several other book projects for **Sugar Maple Press**, including new volumes of the **Living Room Art Gallery Series**, as well as the fifth volume of the Kyle's Bed & Breakfast series.

He can be reached at: gregfox727@gmail.com

His work can be seen at www.kylecomics.com

Thank You!

www.ingramcontent.com/pod-product-compliance
Lightning Source LLC
Chambersburg PA
CBHW050850180526

45159CB00007B/2630